Cathi...

Theresa Argie
"The Haunted Housewives"

i

LOVE BEYOND THE GRAVE

True Tales of Haunted Hearts

THERESA ARGIE & CATHI WEBER
"The Haunted Housewives"

HESTIA MEDIA ♦ OHIO

Cover design by Jake Muelle
Hestia Media Willoughby, Ohio
hestiamedia.com
ISBN-13: 978-0-692-15599-8

ACKNOWLEDGEMENTS

The Haunted Housewives would like to thank, first and foremost, our fans, for believing in us as authors and storytellers. Those who buy our books, come on the ghost walk, attend our lectures, support our fundraisers, or join us on one of our many ghostly adventures - we wouldn't be here without you!

We are grateful to our fellow lovers of history and historic preservation. They see the beauty under the dust and decay and understand the importance of protecting the past.

We salute our ever growing paranormal family - friends who share our passion and appreciate that sometimes you need to stare into the darkness before you can clearly see the light. Together we celebrate our eccentricities.

Next, we would like to thank Michelle Beers for coming to our rescue and editing our original working manuscript in such a timely fashion. (Michelle, the wine we promised you is on the way!)

We want to thank Jeff Belanger for sharing his time and research with us.

We are eternally grateful to Ben Hansen and George Noory for their continued support, especially of our latest project.

And to our dear friend, Michelle Belanger, for writing the forward of this book. Over the years, she has consistently given of her time and talents. Whether it be answering questions on the occult, appearing at one of our fundraisers, or speaking to a group of curious students - Michelle has always managed to come through for us whenever we need her.

Theresa would like to personally thank my partner, Cathi Weber, who is and always will be the "Q" to my "U," the yin to my yang, the Ethel to my Lucy. We simply work better together. You complete me.

And a big heartfelt thanks to my family; J, Elijah, Karen-Mackay, and Jack, for being the light at the end of a very long tunnel. When I write, I sometimes get lost in the words, but my family always helps me find my way back. They are my sounding board, my constructive critics, and my never- ending source of encouragement. My family always seems to know exactly what I need; silence, sleep, coffee, or wine. And yes, it's usually coffee...just kidding, it's wine.

Cathi would like to personally thank my PIC (Partner In Crime), Theresa Argie. Through her I was given a friend who has pushed me to try new things I may never have even considered. Thank you for being blunt and telling me exactly what I need to hear, when I don't want to hear it. Thank you for totally getting my sarcastic sense of humor and dealing with my odd quirks. It's good to have a friend who is just as weird as I am.

Also, I am grateful for my family for supporting me and believing in me even when I sometimes don't believe in myself. They listen to me complain, are patient when I talk nonsense and blurt out things they usually don't comprehend, and attempt to give me sensible advice. Special thanks to Emma and Addy for understanding when Nana had "work" to do.

And last but not least, thanks to my husband, Al, who lovingly indulges my fascination and passion for history and the paranormal, when he is not remotely interested in history - or the paranormal!

FOREWARD

Ghost stories hold a timeless allure, particularly when they are true. That's because good ghost stories aren't merely yarns about the paranormal – they are stories told about people. There is as much pathos as there is terror, and the core of the tale inevitably is the fragile human heart.

Theresa Argie and Cathi Weber understand this, particularly because their careers have followed a path suspended between the identities of historians and paranormal investigators. As researchers, mothers, and grandmothers, birth and death dates are hardly mere numbers. They are the front and back covers of a book – one which they delight in opening and sharing with the world.

In the many tales collected for this volume, hauntings drive the subject of each chapter, but history leads, first and foremost. With meticulous research and concise reporting, Cathi and Theresa set a very human stage with a few strokes of the pen. Places, people, cultural settings – we learn the faces of the major players along with key influences in their lives. More than merely reporting dry details, their curated tour guides us into seeing these individuals with all their complications as people. Through words, the characters come alive for us before we ever encounter hints of their existence beyond death.

Consider the case of Celia Francis Rose, known to her family as "Ceely." For those familiar with Mark Jordan's play of the same name, the end of the story is brutal, sinister and – perhaps – inescapable. But the story first shows us Ceely at her most relatable: a simple-minded Ohio farm girl, mocked for her limitations even by her own kin. Before we learn about Ceely's disconcerting obsessive behaviors, we hear about her dollhouse, her needlepoint, and her hours spent reading the Bible. We see her as a person before we know her as a murderer, and the lightly crafted prose insures that even once we comprehend the full horror and futility of Ceely's selfish plot, we never fully lose sight of that relatable, human spark.

Somewhat harder to make relatable is Harry K. Thaw, a spoiled playboy, addict, and sexual sadist whose obsessions and excesses are almost too big for the page. The husband of famed Gibson Girl, Evelyn Nesbit, Thaw will seem instantly familiar to fans of the television series, American Horror Story through the character of James Patrick March[1]. Larger-than-life in his perfidy, Thaw begs lurid prose and yellow journalism, but the author resists, managing to reveal the full tally of his sins without sliding into sensationalism – a delicate line to navigate, particularly once we get to the details about his real-life whipping boy. And even with such a monster on the page, the tale makes certain the horror does not overshadow the pathos of the chapter's real focus: Evelyn Nesbit herself, a young woman swept up in the tumultuous high society of Gilded Age New York at an age when she was far too easily crafted into both pawn and prey.

Bartered innocence and romantic naïveté continue as themes throughout the book – and perhaps this is

1. [1] It is widely accepted that the character of March was inspired, at least in part, by the real- life H.H. Holmes, an American con-artist and serial killer famed for building a Chicago hotel colloquially referred to as the "Murder Castle." March's plotline with "the Countess," a.k.a. Elizabeth Johnson, echoes elements of the Nesbit/Thaw relationship, however. These echoes are distinct enough to suggest the show-runners also drew inspiration for the pair from the tragic life of the famous Gibson Girl.

intentional commentary on the part of the authors, but it can just as easily be a symptom of the times these stories place beneath the lens. Young women in the nineteenth and early twentieth centuries were rarely in a position to negotiate for their fates, and many were fed confectionary notions on the nature of marriage that left them ill-prepared to deal with reality's bitter taste.

Textile-worker Grace Brown was no exception. A low-born farm girl from South Otselic, New York, she ventured to the city to seek a life beyond tending hens and milking cows. Landing work in a textile factory, she fell unwisely in love with the callous nephew of its owner, a known womanizer. Despite the warnings of family and friends, she gave herself completely to him, ever hopeful that he would make himself her husband.

Once she got pregnant by him, he made himself her murderer instead.

Death is an inescapable outcome in every one of these stories – they wouldn't be ghost stories otherwise. But Theresa and Cathi make those deaths relevant. They call us to bear witness. And the sympathetic lines deftly weaved between reader and subject help to make the final portion of each tale even more gripping. Because, in this book, death is not the final chapter of the tale, not by a long shot. Through Theresa and Cathi, we learn of Grace and Ceely, Evelyn and all the others not simply because they died but because of what came after. Reports of footsteps. Strange sightings. Pale hitchhikers lingering along solitary country lanes not far from old family estates.

Some reports are violent, like the little girl yanked with such force by her hair that she tumbled out of a chair – in a home where sadist Thaw once walked the halls. Figures peer from windows and mirrors, lights flicker and inexplicably go off. As with the historical research, they compile a wealth of accounts, presenting the reports dispassionately yet in a way that leaves the reader intrigued to learn more. As paranormal enthusiasts, Argie and Weber could conceivably use these moments at the end of each chapter for sensation or to proselytize on the existence of ghosts, but they resist on both counts. Instead, they treat these reports with the same conscious aplomb they afford all the lurid details of the marital indiscretions, the domestic manipulations, the murders. With fine, journalistic style, they do not spare the readers, but neither do they lead them.

The end result is a book that reads convincingly as true crime, but with spirits. Even with the copious reports of paranormal phenomenon, history remains the focus – history, meticulously researched, compassionately retold, with its driving force as the people who lived it.

Argie and Weber make it clear that a person's history doesn't always end with the moment of their death. Some stories echo long after the main characters have left the page, and they will suck you right in. I know they did for me.

Michelle Belanger

July 2018

Table of Contents

INTRODUCTION

The American novelist David Foster Wallace penned the phrase, *"**Every love story is a ghost story.**"* He used the quote many times over in his work but never gave an explanation. When drawing a conclusion from the statement, thoughts naturally gravitate towards the many great love stories we've experienced throughout history. Cleopatra and Mark Antony; Samson and Delilah; Napoleon and Josephine; Pocahontas and John Smith. All amazing and enduring love stories...all with tragic endings. Can one conclude, then, that tragedy is the point where a ghostly love story begins?

Tragedy, love, and ghosts are all part of the human condition; interconnected like pieces of a complex puzzle. When powerful emotions refuse to dissipate after bodily death, they leave an unseen residue. This is what fuels a haunting. Ghosts are often the result of tragic events. Sometimes love is the catalyst, sometimes it's the justification. Love is complicated, multifaceted, and difficult to understand. The same can be said of ghosts. There is not one simple definition that completely and accurately illustrates either concept.

There are many different types of love; romantic, tragic, parental, platonic, spiritual, etc. It is an emotional bond not easily broken, even after death. Sometimes love is tainted with morbid obsession or fueled by fiery vengeance.

There are different types of ghosts as well. Examples include residual haunts; spirits that repeat a pattern over and over, like a recording imprinted in the environment. They cannot communicate nor interact with the living. Or the more violent poltergeist, which can manipulate objects in the physical world. They wreak havoc on person and property. They are sourced from a living agent, usually an angst-filled teenager. Then there is the most terrifying category; the demonic or negative entities. These are malevolent beings that never had human form. Their origin comes from a place of darkness and evil.

The ghosts we are most familiar with are the human spirits, those echoes that remain after bodily death. They are the shadows of a person's essence, a splinter of their personality that stays behind after the soul ascends to eternity. Some supernatural force keeps them here on our earthly plane. A ghost might have unfinished business or a message they need to share. They may fear judgment for whatever terrible sins they committed while living. Some seek justice for a past transgression. Some spirits are simply confused and don't realize they are dead.

But some ghosts are created out of an indestructible power that surpasses all others. It does not fade, or wither, or die like flesh. These spirits are unaware of any logic or skepticism that would dismiss their existence. They are emotionally attached to someone or something, tethered by an unbreakable bond of love. Love, in its various forms, is the unseen umbilical cord between the living and the dead.

The following stories revolve around the theme of love and include the elements of a spooky ghost story - passion, suicide, betrayal, and obsession. They were molded and tweaked just so by the storytellers to provide a satisfying connection with you, the reader. A phantom hitchhiker on an endless road, a ghoulish wedding with a corpse bride, a restless spirit that solved its own murder - these are just a few of the essentials in this collection of haunting tales. These are not just ghost stories; they are true historical accountings of people consumed by the power of love.

Love is not an exclusively human experience. An entire chapter of the book is devoted to animals and animal spirits. These are incredible tales of loyalty and love that will make even the most skeptic of reader ponder and give pause...or should we say "paws."

Join these talented storytellers, known as the Haunted Housewives, Theresa Argie and Cathi Weber, as they present some of their favorite ghost stories with a side of history and a heaping of heart. Be it a beautiful haunted passion that resonates beyond death or macabre act of supernatural madness

- these are tales of love beyond the grave.

PATIENT LOVE

Jerusha Howe And Longfellow's Wayside Inn

New England is arguably the most historic area of the United States. It is the birthplace of a fledgling nation that violently, painfully, arose from a pristine land. The majestic wilderness was stained with the blood and tears of those first pioneers who fought native and nature to form the original thirteen colonies. They spread their roots far and wide, creating communities and establishing permanent settlements. Along the rolling countryside, America's forefathers built roads like tributaries that branched out into the unblemished interior of a new world.

Along the well-traveled route known as the Boston Post Road, in a Massachusetts town called Sudbury, sat a way station for weary travelers known as How's Inn. Such places were godsends to those first settlers. The unforgiving terrain and unpredictable weather made even a short journey seem like a monumental odyssey. With only scattered lodgings in the most populated areas, there were few options for those who spent long lonely days on the road.

Built in 1707, How's Inn was the first home to David and Hepz-ibah How and infant son, Ezekiel. In 1716, the inn became a thriving business as well as a family residence. David passed How's Inn to Ezekiel in 1746. Ezekiel How was a Lieutenant Colonel serving the Sudbury Militia during the Revolutionary War.

Ezekiel changed the name from How's Inn to the Red Horse Inn. It was a popular gathering place for social affairs and secret interludes. He held clandestine meetings in the back rooms of his family's inn. Many important military figures frequented the Red Horse. It was a central location for both citizen and soldier during the darkest days of the American Revolution.

After Ezekiel, the Red Horse Inn was handed down to Adam Howe in 1796. It was Adam who added the "e" to the family name, now spelled as Howe. That wasn't the only addition to the family. Each generation of Howes expanded the inn, making needed changes to accommodate the growing business.

Adam passed the Red Horse Inn down to his son, Lyman Howe in 1830. Lyman lived as a bachelor, sharing the inn with his sister, Jerusha. The two were a hospitable pair whose inn was both comfortable and welcoming. Hordes of travelers eagerly made their way to a place where they filled their bellies and rested their weary heads for a night of blissful sleep.

During his time at the helm, Lyman Howe received many notable guests, including poet Henry Wadsworth Longfellow. In 1862, Longfellow sought refuge at the Red Horse while recuper-ating from the devastating loss of his wife in a tragic fire. His personal anguish combined with the bewitching atmosphere of the inn served as inspiration for his most famous work, a collec-tion of poems called Tales of a Wayside Inn.

Longfellow immortalized the building with his haunting prose. He used his pen like an artist's paintbrush, masterfully creating vivid pictures with his words. Although a tale of fiction, Longfellow took creative liberties inspired directly from the people and property that surrounded him during his stay.

He mentioned the inn by name in the prelude, describing the scene with colorful detail. There are several references to ghostly activity in his writing. Was this merely to set the scene? What happened to Longfellow during his stay that compelled him to create his poem? Was it imagination or observation?

> *And, half effaced by rain and shine, The Red Horse prances on the sign. Round this old-fashioned, quaint abode Deep silence reigned, save when a gust Went rushing down the county road, And skeletons of leaves, and dust,*
>
> *A moment quickened by its breath, Shuddered and danced their dance of death, And through the ancient oaks o'erhead Mysterious voices moaned and fled.*
>
> — "Tales Of A Wayside Inn" By Henry Wadsworth Longfellow

As the decades and then centuries passed, the Red Horse Inn changed hands many times. The last Howe to own the property was Lyman Howe. He never married and left no heir, nor did his sister, Jerusha. The property was purchased in 1887 by Edward Lemon, a wool merchant, who intended to reinvent the inn once again. He changed the name from The Red Horse to what we know it as today - Longfellow's Wayside Inn. Lemon wanted to honor the poet whose book shares the name. He envisioned the Wayside Inn to be a gathering place for writers, poets, and other creative types.

3

Lemon invested a sizable amount of money renovating the inn, which was in desperate need of repair. After he died, Lemon's wife sold the property to American industrial giant, Henry Ford. Ford, a documented Freemason, fell in love with the charm and the history of the inn. He was interested in acquiring the Wayside for a special project.

Henry Ford became the owner of the property, part and parcel, from 1923 until 1945. He also purchased 3000 acres of land surrounding the inn. His plan was to expand the current structure and develop a historic village, a preserved piece of Americana, unlike anything the country had seen before. He built eight new buildings on his property, including a grist mill and a chapel. He also had a tiny one-room schoolhouse included in his new community. It was known as the Redstone School, a place for the local children to learn and grow.

In 1928, Henry Ford opened a charter trade school for under-privileged boys: The Wayside Trade School. This replaced the Redstone as the educational facility on his property. Ford's program was designed to give troubled or destitute boys a chance at a better life. These were children that others had given up on, destined for a life of poverty and hardship.

Ford saw the need for intervention and used his wealth and influence to create a lasting legacy. He gave the boys something they never had before; an opportunity to succeed. The young men worked while attending school. They learned a trade that would serve them well in their future. The new skills made the boys eligible to work at Ford's factories in Michigan.

After his death in 1947, Ford willed the property, augmented with additions and renovations, to the state of Massachusetts. He set up a charitable trust for the inn, designating it as a historical museum. Longfellow's Wayside Inn is both the longest continually running inn in the country as well as its first living historical museum.

Much of the property was sold off after Ford's death, but a sizable parcel remained around the inn. A devastating fire in December 1955 nearly destroyed the building forever. If not for the financial trust set up by Ford, the Wayside Inn may have been lost. The structure was rebuilt, preserving as much of its original character as possible. The inn changed hands from the Ford endowment to a board of trustees in 1960. It has been a self-sustaining enterprise ever since.

The Wayside Inn garnered a spot as a Nationally Significant Historic Landmark and Non-Profit in the 1960s. The state of Massachusetts recognized the district in 1967. The inn stands as a testament to Americana and a tribute to our country's history.

The inn never stopped welcoming overnight guests and history buffs. Those who ran the Wayside worked hard to keep the legacy alive. The savvy innkeepers took a cue from the past to ensure a bright future.

In the 1950s, proprietor Francis Koppeis searched for an interesting way to drum up business. Inspiration came after he discovered tiny secret compartments in one of the inn's antique desks. For centuries, hidden drawers were a common way to hide one's valuables from would-be robbers. Money, jewelry, property deeds, wills - all could be safely stashed away from prying eyes. It was the common man's safe deposit box.

Koppeis entertained visitors, especially children, with stories of the hidden drawers in the inn's desks. He turned the story into a clever game similar to a scavenger hunt. The children foraged for treasures through the building, searching for secret cubby holes and nooks filled with candy and small treats. This eventually morphed into an adult practice of leaving letters and messages instead of candy. The hidden drawers were used for surreptitious note passing. Whether for secret love letters outlining salacious plans or just fun games of hide-and-go-seek, the idea of the Secret Drawer Society was born.

The phenomenon of the Secret Drawer Society took hold and continues today as a cherished tradition. Visitors often leave notes hidden in drawers, walls, floorboards, and just about anywhere someone could stash a piece of paper. Over the years, hundreds, if not thousands, of notes have been written, hidden, discovered, and replaced. Not all notes outline dark deeds or confessions of love. Many recount the various paranormal experiences had while staying at the Longfellow's Wayside Inn. The most interesting notes by far are those written to or about Jerusha Howe.

Jerusha Howe, the sister of Lyman, was the last Howe to own the inn. She was born 1797 and lived with her brother all her life. Since Lyman never married, Jerusha was fundamental in the success of the business. She helped with the crucial duties of running the inn; cooking, cleaning, and being cordial and accommodating. She was a welcoming figure to those who sought respite at the popular establishment.

Running the Red Horse was a fulltime job. Lyman How was grateful for his sister's help. Jerusha was a faithful companion to her brother. She kept busy with the day-to-day life of an innkeeper, never complaining, never thinking of herself. She focused on keeping the guests happy. Secretly her heart ached, but she quietly accepted her mundane existence and suffered her lonely life in silence.

Jerusha was known as "The Belle of Sudbury." She was warm and welcoming, a fine young woman who charmed everyone around her. She had a beautiful voice and was very talented musically. She owned the first pianoforte in town and often entertained guests with her musical prowess.

Though she enjoyed the attention when performing, Jerusha was usually one to stay out of the spotlight. She was said to be timidly beautiful and painfully modest. There's no doubt she caught the eye of many men who stayed at the Red Horse. Some travelers made trips to the inn just to be in her company. They may have imagined what a fine wife she would make.

Although friendly and courteous, Jerusha kept all suitors at a distance. Either oblivious or unimpressed, she never gave much thought to male guests who tried to court her. Jerusha wanted something more. She wanted true love, forever love - the kind poets write sonnets about. Although countless men pursued her romantically, none captured her heart.

One fateful day Jerusha's life changed forever. Although the exact names and dates have been lost to history, those who know the tale agree that Jerusha's story is one of love, heartache, and loss.

On that day a handsome stranger, supposedly an English-man, walked through the doors of the Wayside Inn. He was quiet and weary from the road. Jerusha could see his chiseled features and sparkling eyes under the layers of dust he shook from his clothes. He was possibly a merchant or a soldier, stopping by on route to the big city. Little is known of his exact origins or intentions.

The stranger had a certain charisma that Jerusha couldn't ignore. She was immediately enchanted. This man was different. She could feel her heart flutter as he spoke; his accent like a melody to her ears. The usually articulate Jerusha found herself momentarily speechless. The Englishman couldn't help but notice Jerusha, her cheeks full and flush, her smile a welcoming beacon in the dark New England night. He too felt the intense charge of excitement as he lay down his traveling case.

Jerusha was enamored. For the first time in her life she was absolutely smitten. The mysterious Englishman felt the same, or so it seemed. They began a romantic, albeit brief love affair. For a time, the couple was happy, carrying on like two people in love. There were romantic rendezvous in dark corners, whispered promises and stolen kisses. Jerusha felt the electric twinge of passion whenever their hands touched.

Oh, how happy Jerusha was! These were the most exciting days of her life. She saw a future for herself beyond the confines of the family business. No longer was she bound as the dutiful hostess, sister of the innkeeper. Jerusha believed the relationship would lead to marriage. The intentions of the mysterious Englishman can only be conjectured.

And then one day, Jerusha's suitor was gone. She believed the separation was temporary; that her betrothed was off making preparations for their future. He vowed to come back as soon as possible. Jerusha fully expected her lover to return and take her away from the lonely, banal life at the Wayside.

But the mysterious stranger that captured her pure and gentle heart never came back. The Englishman walked out the door of the Wayside Inn and was never heard from again. Jerusha had no idea that "goodbye" was forever. The missing pieces of the puzzle have been filled in over time by speculation. It is possible that the Englishman left to make wedding arrangements. Maybe he had some business to attend to before he could bring his bride back to England. But other theories paint a darker picture.

One assumption states the man had no intention of marrying Jerusha. He considered his time with her at the Wayside nothing but a fling. Maybe he was already married and left Jerusha to return to his wife back in his home country. Perhaps he "moved on" or met another woman. Others speculate he was truly in love with her. He planned to return as soon as possible, but fate cruelly intervened. He met with an unexpected event, some terrible tragedy on the way back to England. He may have drowned in a shipwreck or ran into some nefarious pirate types.

We will never know the fate of the Englishman, but Jerusha's fate was sealed. She would never love another. Jerusha yearned for her beau to return. With every knock on the door and every letter delivered to the inn, she prayed it would be news from her beloved. Jerusha pined for her sweetheart, holding fast to the idea that he would come back to her one day. It was destiny. While she waited, Jerusha hid her pain behind a smile and rarely let sadness interfere with the business of running the inn. For years she went on like that, her heart breaking a little bit more each passing day.

Eventually, after what felt like an eternity, Jerusha faced the fact that her lover would not be coming back. She was completely and utterly devastated. Jerusha would never find love again. She refused to abandon her brother, Lyman, as keeper of the inn. She buried her pain so deep that the emotions burned a hole in her soul. Her emotional agony destroyed her from the inside. Once a healthy and vibrant young woman with everything to live for, Jerusha was now apathetic and dispassionate. She wanted only to escape this mortal coil. Those who knew her best say Jerusha died of a broken heart. She was only forty-five years old.

Jerusha Howe haunts the Longfellow's Wayside Inn. Her lovelorn spirit has been seen in the halls, the restaurant, and in the guest rooms. She tends to favor rooms 9 and 10, the rooms thought to be her sleeping quarters when she was alive.

Guests staying in the inn report hearing the soft sobs of a woman in despair. Others claim they hear childlike laughter maybe Jerusha from a happier time? The sound of the pianoforte carries its sweet melody throughout the inn. It is thought to be Jerusha, still entertaining visitors.

People report the wispy apparition of a female form whisk by them in the halls. They see someone matching Jerusha's description standing at the foot of their beds in the middle of the night. Although at first frightening, an overwhelming sense of calm soon emerges. Some guests feel the sensation of being watched, even during "private" moments. It's as if you are never alone at the Wayside Inn. Visitors smell Jerusha's signature citrus perfume for a brief moment before it inexplicably dissipates into thin air.

The most incredible paranormal encounters are documented in the many letters and notes tucked carefully away in hidden drawers and hiding places, courtesy of participants in the Secret Drawer Society. Some leave notes for Jerusha, telling her to hold on or to let go. They offer sympathetic support for the heartsick woman centuries after the love affair ended.

Another well-documented phenomenon is the unwanted attention that male visitors get from Jerusha's ghost. Her unmis takable presence clamors for attention from the men staying at the inn. They report the sensation of being touched or caressed by a gentle female phantom. They feel soft, ethereal kisses on the face or delicate ghostly hands on their skin. Some men claim they feel someone unseen crawl into bed with them as they sleep.

Some people categorized Jerusha Howe as a succubus; a spirit that feeds off the sexual energy of the living. Although this sounds incredibly macabre, her affections are not entirely unwell come. She means no harm. She is a sad and sympathetic figure just aching to be loved.

Jerusha may simply be tired of waiting. Centuries of disappointment and despair have turned the broken-hearted woman into a frisky spirit longing for the physical and emotional attention she was robbed of in life. The Longfellow's Wayside Inn is haunted by the lovelorn spirit of a lonely girl. If you're ever a guest the inn, leave Jerusha a note. And remember, even the empty rooms may be otherworldly occupied.

YOUNG LOVE

The Story Of Minnie Quay

Young Minnie Quay, so pretty and fair
A girl who could tempt you with a toss of her hair

With a smile that attracted the strongest of men
And eyes with the soul of the moon and the wind.

— From The Song, "The Ghost Of Minnie Quay" By Jory Brown, 2005.

James and Mary Ann Quay, along with their eldest daughter, Mary Jane (known as Minnie), son Samuel, and baby girl, Amanda, left New York to settle in the village of Forester, Michigan, around the year 1870.

Forester was a fishing community located right on the shoreline of Lake Huron. The dense forests of this area presented economic opportunities that could not be ignored. Local lumber mills and the fisheries were thriving in the mid-1800s.

Logging was the main industry in Forester. Along with this burgeoning industry came the various needs of a self-supporting town. A large general store, post office, boarding houses, sawmill, blacksmith, shingle mill and a cooper were all part of the busy existence in the little town on the lake. The completion of Smith's Dock in 1859 gave rise to the village as a significant port on Lake Huron.

Smith's Dock was considered a masterpiece of engineering at such an early time in this young nation. The massive dock continued for nearly 1000 feet out into Lake Huron. The pilings were sunk deep into the bedrock of the lake. Perhaps the intent for those timber pillars was to ensure they could continue their job into the present day. It was a wide wharf with plenty of room for the four long warehouses they constructed. The dock clearly represented the town's commitment to the shipping industry; the sturdy construction cemented their relationship with the vessels that traveled the Great Lakes. Large schooners and steamships could moor there with little difficulty. It came that life in this town revolved around milled lumber and the ships needed to carry it.

As a veteran of the Civil War, James Quay was granted land in Forester as payment for his service. It so happened that he had a brother named David who lived in the area. David encouraged James to relocate, outlining the many virtues of the great state. After careful consideration, James made the decision to move his family to Michigan. The promise of a job in one of the plentiful lumber mills provided incentive.

Shortly after arriving, James secured a job as a mechanic in the local saw mill. The Quay family continued to grow as they settled into life in Forester. Mary Ann gave birth to a daughter, Lauraette, in 1870 followed by son James in 1871. When baby Charles arrived in 1874, the family was complete.

Minnie, as the eldest daughter, would have had a very predictable life. She spent her days helping her mother by caring for her younger siblings, preparing meals, and doing chores. Longing for more, Minnie had her mind on life outside of her insulated world. A prosperous and energetic port would be of interest to any child, and Minnie was no different. She visited the dock where excitement was the norm. Ships from distant shores, passenger and cargo alike, transporting both travelers and goods, would converge there. The colorful life of a harbor town calmed the soul of a girl with wanderlust in her heart.

For a young girl in the late 1800's, education ended early. Minnie was considered formally educated at the age of 15 and was no longer required to go to school. She bloomed into a strikingly beautiful young woman. She was the envy of other girls her age because of her looks.

Minnie enjoyed a solitary existence, keeping to herself. She enjoyed spending time getting caught up in a good book. The young girl's soul seemed to find pleasure outdoors. Whenever she had some unexpected free time, nature is where she could be found. She liked to go for long, thoughtful walks along the waterfront, and Smith's dock was an overpowering draw.

Much to her parents' displeasure, Minnie took every opportunity to wander down to the harbor. Her mother and father feared she might encounter a sinister and disreputable sailor, and they forbid her to visit the dock. It was during one of these secretive visits to the port that Minnie, with her carefree and rebellious nature, met a young sailor who captured her heart.

History has never revealed the name of the sailor, nor the exact ship on which he served. The people of Forester seemed to know she had a faithful commitment to meet this mysterious merchant man of the sea each time his ship anchored at Smith's Dock. This tryst was witnessed and confirmed by many of the town's folk and it set tongues to wagging.

Eventually, word got back to James and Mary Ann Quay, and they became furious! Minnie had openly disobeyed them, so they took every measure they could to ensure she would never stray again. Whenever her suspected lover was in port, Minnie was unceremoniously locked in her room. She could see the dock from her bedroom windows, but could not reach out to her sweetheart to tell him why she could not meet him. Her isolation was complete each time she glimpsed his ship's flag at the water's edge. Minnie worried he might assume she had abandoned him.

Time passed slowly and winter set in. The ships no longer visited the harbor during the icy storms and gales. Minnie's heart ached for her handsome sailor, and these wistful feelings almost consumed her. The frigid air seeped into the heart of Minnie Quay. Her despair heightened greatly during the bleak winter months. She was at last freed from the prison of her room and once again able to wander the now empty dock.

Minnie found the gray, watery light that shone during the daytime to be depressing. The barren, frozen expanse over the water offered a harsh reality to the longing she had for the warmth of her lover's embrace. The crystalline ice formations on the glistening, frozen landscape once held endless fascination for Minnie. She now viewed them with vacant, staring eyes.

A feeling of dread seemed to overcome Minnie. She was frightened she might never see the man she yearned for again. She pulled her cape closer as a bleak and blustery wind whipped through the bitter cold. The snow crunched crisply under her fleeting feet as she walked home feeling dejected. Her tears of longing remained, frozen on her cheeks.

Winter never lasts forever. Spring follows; a season full of hope and renewal. When the thaw came, Minnie was once again filled with joy and a sense of purpose. She made the decision to visit the port whenever she could safely sneak away. While there, she relentlessly asked anyone and everyone for news of the ship that carried her sailor. Often met with grunts and angry gestures, Minnie remained resolute. She continued her investigation with a vengeance that only a woman in love could fully understand.

Records reveal that in late November of 1875, one of the worst storms of the decade unexpectedly arose. It unleashed all the power of an arctic high- pressure system over the Great Lakes. The gale-force winds and deadly below-zero temperatures, with driving ice and snow, made this situation a death sentence for any ships that happened upon the lake when it hit. During the harshness of the storm, Minnie had spent hours worrying about the fate of her cherished merchantman.

Minnie never wavered from her quest for news of her sweetheart. On April 27, 1876, after days of fruitlessly searching for an answer, she happened upon a sailor who could tell her with certainty the whereabouts of her beloved. And the report he gave her was devastating. Minnie was told the ship carrying her sailor sunk in one of the lake's harsh and unyielding winter storms. The man was certain the ship had foundered and all aboard had perished. The storms of November captured the lives of many sailors that year.

The icy waters had claimed her one true love. Learning of his untimely death, Minnie was driven to the brink of insanity. Her grief devoured her as she staggered aimlessly towards home. She changed into her best dress, a long light-colored gown. She told her little brother to be good and stay put as she left the house.

Minnie closed the door with a snap of finality; the fate of her decision looming before her.

With leaden feet, Minnie began her final journey towards Smith's Dock. People sitting on the porch of the nearby Tanner House watched as she passed by, waving to her retreating figure. But no one was prepared for the shocking sight that next greeted them. With unwavering determination, Minnie continued down the dock to the very end of the pier, paused for a brief moment, then jumped into the dark, cold waters of Lake Huron.

The following appeared in the Detroit Free Press the next day, April 28, 1876: *Port Huron, April 27 - A young girl named Minnie Quay, about fifteen years of age, committed suicide by throwing herself into the lake from Smith's Dock, at Forester, Michigan this afternoon. She was seen in the act of jumping by her little brother, who was on shore. A quick alarm was given, and men commenced at once to grapple for the body, but it was an hour before it was recovered. Her father is a mechanic in Smith's mill, and is highly respected. No cause is assigned for this rash act.*

Minnie's death was officially listed as "suicide by drowning." The lake is dangerous at any time of the year, but especially in the early springtime. The spring weather might have felt warm on that April day, but the typical temperature of the water would have still been below 40 degrees Fahrenheit.

When Minnie jumped into the frigid water, her first involuntary gasp for air would have caused her to aspirate and swallow water. Panic would have been followed by shock and Minnie's muscles would stop functioning. She would no longer have been able to save herself. Hypothermia sets in and drowning occurs, all within a matter of minutes. One has to wonder, did

18

Minnie's strong will to join her love hold her under the water? Perhaps the thought of joining him at the bottom of the lake brought her some relief from the bitter pain and anguish of his loss.

As the town of Forester recovered from the shock of the young girl's drowning, the ghostly tales of Minnie Quay began. She was seen wandering the lonely shore in a flowing white gown. Her moans and cries, together with the crashing waves, echoed through the souls of those who glimpsed the apparition. Many of the townsfolk claim to have witnessed Minnie standing in the pounding surf of the lake, calling out to those on shore to join her in her watery grave. The town of Forester was haunted by the ghost of Minnie Quay.

Through the years, many of these ghost tales have been well documented and discussed at length in the newspapers. In the late 1980s, the new owner of the abandoned Forester Inn claimed it was haunted by the ghost of Minnie Quay. He alleged she had been seen in a long white dress wandering through the rooms of the inn. He also claimed to have the best steak dinner around. This caused quite a stir!

Soon after, busloads of people began to arrive at the inn to dine, to wander around the beaches of Lake Huron, and to stroll through the cemetery, all in an effort to meet the spirit of Minnie Quay. It got so bad that at one point streets of this small rural town were clogged with visitors, and the police had to be called to help with crowd control. The owner of the inn was accused of creating a hoax to bring tourists to his restaurant. Soon, a local psychic medium began to hold séances, for a fee. Participants would attempt to contact Minnie to ask her spirit to speak with them. There were organized searches of the graveyard and the shoreline, in hopes of finding evidence of the young girl's ghost.

A local relative of the Quay family was interviewed for a newspaper article about the ghost of Minnie Quay. She purported she still lived directly across the street from the Quay family home, and made some dubious claims. While inside the family homestead she reported seeing pottery fly off the shelf for no apparent reason. The vacuum turned on by itself one day while she cleaned. The pendant lights would suddenly swing of their own volition. She would hear raps and bangs when in the house alone. She was convinced that Minnie was there, and her spirit would never rest.

To this day people still seek her ghost. The internet is rife with stories of ghost hunters trying to find out for themselves if the spirit of Minnie Quay still stalks the shores of Lake Huron. It seems as if she is destined to pine for her beloved eternally; a sailor lost at sea who will never return. There are claims that Minnie seeks young women who've suffered similar heartbreak. Her deceptive spirit beckons them to join her in the frigid lake waters. Minnie's specter has also been sighted hovering over the isolated shoreline, issuing anguished cries which have reached the ears of many. Others report that if you are brave enough to wander through the Forester Cemetery at nightfall, you will discover the ghost of Minnie Quay weeping over her own grave.

The small town of Forester is no longer recognized as a port town. There is an old inn, with honey gold paneling on the walls, and deer and moose heads mounted over the bar. The cemetery where Minnie Quay and her family are buried still exists. And there on the lake, the remnants of Smith's Dock can still be seen, jutting out of the lake like proud sailors. The wood pilings stand in tribute to the young girl whose legend and stories continue to haunt the town long after after her tragic death.

Young Love

So out on a pier, with a stormy lake screaming.
She stared at the water where her lover lay
sleeping

And the undertow grabbed her as she entered
the cold She drew her last breath, and gave up
her soul.

So, just after midnight, the waves at her feet She
walks by the water, a tale bittersweet

From the waters of Huron, she beckons it's told
With lips ever tempting, and eyes icy cold.

— From The Song, "The Ghost Of
Minnie Quay" By Jory Brown, 2005.

SECRET LOVE

Ladelle Allen

Monticello, Arkansas is a picturesque slice of Americana. It's a small town with a respectable university, a plethora of churches, and well-established neighborhoods. Nestled among white picket fences and mature trees, sits a majestic Victorian structure known as the Allen House. The building is a mix of Gothic, Neoclassical, and Queen Anne architectural styles. It takes the most interesting features of each to create one of the most spectacular homes in all of Arkansas.

Built between 1905 and 1906, The Allen House was the home of Joe Lee Allen and his family. The grand mansion was a gift for Joe Allen's wife, Caddye, and their children; daughters Lonnie Lee, Ladelle, and Lewie. The Allen's infant son, Walter, died nearly a decade before they moved into the new house.

The Allen House was a fitting tribute to the success of Joe Allen. His entrepreneurial ventures included investments, hotel ownership, and horse and buggy sales. He had a hand in the fledgling automotive industry and was president of the Commercial Loan and Trust

Company. Allen's wealth afforded the family a lavish and comfortable lifestyle. Their Monticello mansion was exactly what Joe Allen hoped it would be; "the most impressive house in town."

The Allen family were as close to royalty as one could get in Monticello at the time. Their social status was secure and their reputation beyond reproach. Caddye, an exceptional hostess, threw the best parties in town. These lavish affairs were always the highlight of the season and everyone yearned to be on the guest list. Exquisite samplings of savory delights followed by choice wines and delicious liqueurs were always on the menu, as well as jovial music and engaging conversation.

The three Allen girls enjoyed a privileged upbringing. Their future was as open and bright as the Arkansas sky. Ladelle, the middle daughter, was beautiful and well educated, with a natural grace and charm. She was confident, vivacious, and admired by all who met her. She had no shortage of suitors, but Ladelle struggled to find true love.

It surprised everyone when Ladelle wed Boyd Randolph Bonner in 1914. Boyd was a billiard hall owner and oil rig worker with a tarnished reputation. He was crass and impetuous, but had an undeniable charisma. He was a poor match for such a refined young woman, but Ladelle was drawn to his provocative bad boy image. Despite opposition from her family, Ladell and Boyd married. Exactly one year later, the couple welcomed a son, Elliott Allen Bonner, aka Allen.

In 1917, the patriarch of the family, Joe Lee Allen passed away suddenly at age fifty-four. Merriment gave way to melancholy as a dark cloud settled over the Allen women. Ladelle took the death particularly hard. She was extremely close to her father. A series of unfortunate events followed that zapped the spirit of the once vibrant Ladelle.

Ladelle and Boyd struggled to keep their marriage together. They relocated several times over the next two decades, going from Arkansas to Texas to Memphis. The multiple moves only compounded their marital problems. In 1927, Ladelle and Boyd divorced. Ladelle sought solace in the only place she felt safe; her family home in Arkansas.

Although the marriage fell apart, their son Allen seemed to thrive. He was intelligent, ambitious, and had a commendable lust for life. He enjoyed a successful academic career and had no trouble finding work after graduation. In 1944, Allen found himself in New York City working for the Associated Press.

Tragedy struck when young Allen contracted pneumonia. The illness was quick and consuming. After languishing for a week and a half, Elliot Allen Bonner died. He was only twenty-eight years old. Ladelle was devastated. The loss of her only son was emotionally crippling.

Death wasn't finished with the Allen family. It next aimed its sight on Ladelle's younger sister, Lewie. Lewie took ill unexpectedly and died eight months after Ladelle buried her son. She was only forty-six years old.

Ladelle's personal tragedies compounded as the years went on. She was plagued by alcoholism and bouts of depression. Even with all the luxuries of wealth and privilege, she couldn't find happiness. Money couldn't heal the hole in her heart nor the pain encapsulating her soul. But a chance encounter with an old beau changed her life forever.

In March of 1948, Ladelle was unexpectedly reunited with her high school sweetheart, Prentiss Hemingway Savage. They were once the envy of all their classmates, a teenage power couple. Circumstance ended their romance, but they parted on good terms. Ladelle was delighted to see Prentiss again. Thirty-five years after their last date, fate fortuitously thrust the former flames together once more. The timing was incredible. Ladelle was broken and lonely until Prentiss literally knocked on her front door.

Prentiss, an executive for Texaco Oil, was a wealthy businessman who referred to himself as a "wolf." He respected the canine predator for its stealth and strength. This was the inspiration for his personal and professional prowess. He was handsome, confident, and socially Ladelle's equal. The reunion between Ladelle and Prentiss was a welcome distraction. Both felt a familiar spark. They were like teenagers, filled with jocularity and exhilaration. The only obstacle blocking the couple's rekindled romance was that Prentiss was very much a married man.

Ladelle would not let this inconvenient little detail be a hindrance. She and Prentiss had a connection stronger than circumstance or time. She had suffered enough, lost too much. Now her spirit was rejuvenated. This was a second chance, maybe her last chance, at happiness. Thus began a passionate and secret love affair that would end with Ladelle's untimely death.

On December 26th, 1949, Ladelle Allen Bonner intentionally consumed a lethal dose of mercury cyanide. The poison slowly, painfully worked through her body irreparably damaging her internal organs. Ladelle lingered on her deathbed for days while her family and friends tried to understand why she would do such a drastic and irreversible thing. Although she had been depressed for some time, she seemed happier in the preceding months. Feeling puzzled, her family wondered why she chose suicide. And why now? They were unaware of Ladelle's secret affair with Prentiss.

The series of events that led up to Ladelle's death finally came to light sixty years later. In August of 2009, the current owners of the Allen House, Mark and Rebecca Spencer, discovered eighty three letters hidden beneath the attic floor. The letters were addressed to Ladelle, most from Prentiss Hemingway Savage, who signed the letters "P" or "X."

The letters were as fragile as Ladelle's broken heart; aged and discolored, filled with glimmers of hope and the foreshadowing of inevitable tragedy. They were a window into the damaged soul of a lovelorn woman, desperate for something that would never come.

Paranormal happenings preceded the discovery of the letters by decades, long before the Spencers set foot on the property. It was no secret to anyone in Monticello that the Allen House was haunted. The old Victorian was the stuff of urban legends, complete with exaggerated rumors and compelling half- truths. But locals swore that the house was teeming with ghosts.

Ghost sightings were commonplace and continual since the late 1940s. Pale female faces peered out of empty bedroom windows. The spirits of three young girls played happily in the foyer, oblivious to any living occupants in the home. There was also a compelling photograph from the 1960s of a ghostly figure hovering in the Allen House dining room. A vast array of supernatural manifestations were known to inhabit the dwelling, along with a very "spirited" caretaker.

Rumors of a haunting didn't deter the Spencer family from relentlessly trying to buy the Allen House. They figured any historic Victorian home was bound to be a source of ghostly gossip. It was part of the charm and allure of what Rebecca Spencer referred to as her "dream house." The eccentricity of the current owner and resident only added to the home's mystique.

The owner was an odd woman, reluctant to sell a home she dearly loved. She openly admitted the house was haunted. She thwarted Mark and Rebecca's initial approach. It took some effort just to get a foot in the door, literally. Eventually, they convinced the owner to meet with them and discuss the possibility of selling. The negotiations felt more like an audition. It was as if the house had to choose its new owner, not the other way around.

Mark and Rebecca's tenacity and patience finally paid off. The Spencers purchased the house in June of 2007. They quickly discovered the whispers of a haunting were true. The bizarre happenings began as soon as the Spencers moved in, even before they were unpacked. Subtle at first, the events seemed harmless, almost playful. But some things were more unsettling.

Rebecca and Mark noted the odd behavior of their youngest son, Jacob. At times, he was despondent or unusually quiet. Sometimes he appeared to be in two places at once. They saw him standing stoically in a doorway one moment, but then suddenly disappear the next. They were surprised to discover that Jacob was actually in a completely different part of the house at the time.

Mark and Rebecca chalked these sightings up to fatigue and the stress of moving. But the peculiar phenomenon continued. The strange activity compounded when they began renovating. Overwhelming feelings of sadness plagued Rebecca, feelings she knew were not her own. Crying sounds echoed in unoccupied rooms, ominous shadows peeked from darkened corners. There was the heavy and constant sensation that they were not alone. It was evident that someone or something shared the old Victorian with the Spencer family.

Curiosity seekers often knocked on their door asking for a tour of the "haunted" Allen House. The audacity of these strangers both amused and inspired them. Their home's ghostly reputation was well earned and the Spencers decided to use this to their advantage.

On Halloween night 2007, the Mark and Rebecca

opened their home to the public. They offered a historic guided tour, charging a nominal fee to help offset the ever-increasing renovation costs. Locals finally had an opportunity to see inside the legendary Allen House and hear the haunted history first hand.

The response was overwhelming. Hundreds of people showed up that first October evening. Some came to see the renovations, but most hoped to catch a glimpse of one of the house's ghostly inhabitants. People reported bizarre paranormal happenings that first night. Guests felt an eerie presence as they walked the mansion's halls. Some thought the Spencers staged the spooky activity to enhance the experience. They did not.

The feedback confirmed what Mark and Rebecca already knew. The Allen House was haunted. This laid the foundation for further research and investigations. For the next two years, the Spencer family lived side by side with the spirits of the Allen House. The identity of the ghosts remained a mystery until one hot August day in 2009. It was then that the pieces of the puzzle fell into place.

On that particular morning, Mark felt a supernatural pull to "treasure hunt" in the attic. Guided by a voice inside his head, he knew he'd find something interesting. Mark was compelled, if not led, to a spot near the south turret where he made a remarkable discovery. Between the weathered floorboards, under decades of dust and darkness, was the answer to the mysteries of the Allen House. From the void of the attic floor, Mark pulled up a large brown envelope. The writing outside was legible but faded. Inside were smaller envelopes containing love letters postmarked 1948, addressed to L.A. Bonner.

Ladelle Allen Bonner

Mark was astounded and excited all at once. Carefully, he opened each envelope revealing faded words written in neat prose. One by one he read the letters. They were from Prentiss Hemingway Savage to his lover Ladelle Allen Bonner. Although he had only half of the conversation, he easily pieced together the story. Mark could read the powerful emotions buried between the lines of each correspondence.

The words written were innocent at first, a bit of flirting and reminiscing. As he read on, Mark could sense the intensity growing with each letter. It was much more than just small talk and friendly banter. It was clear Ladelle and Prentiss were in love. Each letter revealed the escalating passion of two lovers, separated by insurmountable circumstances. Prentiss professed his true love and burning desire to be with Ladelle. The couple made plans for their future. Ladelle Allen Bonner, who was then fifty-four, finally found the love she had searched for all her life.

The letters laid out a timeline for the two reunited lovebirds. After some time and careful planning, Prentiss and Ladelle spent a passionate week in Ontario, Canada. There they were free to express their desires and consummate their relationship. The physical pleasures were nothing compared to the emotional ecstasy for Ladelle. She was never happier. Prentiss showered her with affection, promises, and hope.

They had one looming obstacle in the way of their future, the current Mrs. Prentiss Savage. Ladelle didn't want to be "the other woman," she wanted to be Prentiss' wife. It was imperative that he get a divorce. His listless marriage was a roadblock to their happiness.

Only months after their passionate tryst in Canada, things started to fall apart. A dark reality clouded the relationship. Prentiss told Ladelle that divorcing his wife was not going to be as easy as expected. It was fraught with unforeseen financial and personal difficulties. He feared damaging his reputation with a scandal as well as losing most of his fortune.

Ladelle was devastated. She didn't care about his money, only his love. It was as if he pulled the rug out from under her. She was dizzy and numb. Her heart ached at the thought of losing Prentiss. She started a free fall into despair that would end with a thundering crash. It was glaringly clear Prentiss was never going to leave his wife.

Mark Spencer could tell by the dates that the letters were coming less and less frequently. Instead of planning their future, it was a discussion of the obstacles Prentiss faced with a divorce. It was one reason or another. The letters were no longer confessions of love; they were just small talk and excuses.

Ladelle sank deeper and deeper into depression. This was her last chance at true love, and it was rapidly slipping away. Loneliness was her constant companion. Ladelle couldn't bear another holiday without her love, without the hope for the future. She knew Prentiss would never fulfill his promise.

On Christmas night, 1948, Caddye Allen entertained guests at one of her lavish affairs. While everyone celebrated, Ladelle silently suffered. She could no longer pretend to be happy. Her heart was breaking and she had no one to talk to, no one with whom to share her frustration and sadness. Ladelle excused herself from the party and retreated to her bedroom with grave intentions. Alone and defeated, she drank a deadly cocktail laced with mercury cyanide.

Ladelle Allen Bonner died on January 2, 1949.

Now it was clear. Mark Spencer had at long last solved the sixty-year mystery of Ladelle's suicide. It was the thought of living without Prentiss, of living a life devoid of love and passion. She was tired of waiting forever for something that would never come to pass.

The emotions tied to Ladelle's death fueled the paranormal happenings at the Allen House. Ladelle was still there, haunting the one place she felt truly safe and loved. This was where she spent the best years of her life and the place where she dreamed of a future that was not meant to be. She wasn't alone anymore. Ladelle joined the band of ghostly spirits that chose to stay in the old Victorian.

Rebecca Spencer had visions of a ghostly woman whom she now believed to be Ladelle. She empathically felt her pain and suffering. Ladelle's spirit reached out to Rebecca, someone who understood the power of love. She wanted to connect to a sympathetic woman with whom she felt a kinship, someone kind and forgiving - someone who wouldn't judge her for loving a married man.

The Spencers finally had an answer and the physical proof to back it up. The letters told the story of Ladelle's heartache and why she felt suicide was her only option. They were also clues to why the house was so haunted. Mark and Rebecca were chosen to unravel this mystery and they wanted to share their findings with the world.

The Allen House opened for both historic tours and paranormal investigations in 2008. The Spencers had an important duty to fulfill. They would expose, yet honor the legacy of Ladelle Allen Bonner and her family by telling her story.

Mark Spencer wrote a book, A Haunted Love Story: The Ghosts of the Allen House, in 2012. He chronicles the history of the home and the people who lived there. He details the discovery of the letters and the current happenings on his property.

Ladelle's letters could have been discovered by any one of the home's previous owners. It wasn't until the

Spencers came along that the truth finally revealed itself to the world. Ladelle chose Mark and Rebecca to be the keepers of the memories.

The paranormal activity guided them to the remarkable discovery in the attic. They have lived side by side with ghosts since they moved into the Allen House. They've not only accepted the activity, but they've learned to embrace it.

Paranormal encounters continue at the home. Some of the most telling incidents of ghostly activity included strange electrical occurrences, EMF spikes, light anomalies, disembodied voices, and countless EVPs (electronic voice phenomena). These are chilling voices of the dead that imprint themselves on recording devices. Rebecca recalled having her hair pulled by phantom hands.

Most disturbing was the behavior of their young son, Jacob, who appeared to be in two places at once. This doppelgänger phenomenon was particularly unsettling. Sometimes he had uncharacteristic mood swings. Once he told his parents, "I'm not Jacob anymore."

Mark and Rebecca keep track of the paranormal activity in the home. Ghostly faces appear in windows. Phantom cigar smells loft through the air. Doors latch and unlatch themselves. A female apparition wanders the hallways of the Allen House. This may be Ladelle, or it may be another one of the home's other worldly residents.

Several paranormal teams have investigated the home. They've all had unexplainable experiences. They concur there are many spirits in the Allen House, but not all have been identified. The Spencers believe they are most likely members of the same family, including Caddye, Ladelle's devoted mother and matriarch of the Allen family.

But it is the EVPs that seem the most telling. One

group of investigators captured a woman's voice that said, "I lied." Another ghostly voice exclaimed, "I don't like it here." One night, while Rebecca and a paranormal team discussed the newly found letters in the attic, they captured an EVP that said, "They would reveal us." Mark Spencer says that was the loudest, clearest EVP ever captured in the Allen House.

And how true it was. The letters revealed the love affair between Prentiss Hemingway Savage and Ladelle Allen Bonner. Ladelle, a respected figure in society, was willing to compromise her reputation and her virtue so as to have a chance at true love. In the end, she paid for her sins with her life. But her soul remains behind, wandering the meticulously restored halls of her Monticello mansion, still searching for the happiness that eluded her in life and leaving a ghostly residue behind.

FOOL FOR LOVE

Kate Morgan, The Beautiful Stranger

In late November of 1892, a mysterious young woman showed up at a posh California hotel with no luggage and no chaperone. Over the course of her stay, the woman's actions and demeanor raised many eyebrows. By the fifth day, her odd behavior crescendoed. In a tumultuous moment of deep despair, she took her own life. Her ghost lives on in the telling and retelling of her final days. She is known to many at the Hotel Del Coronado as "The Beautiful Stranger," and her spirit has never checked out.

Many paranormal enthusiasts may be familiar with the story of Kate Morgan and the ghosts of the Hotel Del Coronado. It has been high on the Haunted Housewives' ghost hunting bucket list for years. But as we delved deeper into the legend and history surrounding this reputed haunting, we discovered an amalgamation. It often happens that facts and reputations don't always sync. Truth can be stranger than fiction. The theories and myths about this ghost are far more intriguing than we ever imagined. Thanks to some stellar investigation by a former Del Coronado employee, detailed record keeping by the hotel, combined with our own luck in finding the research, we offer some compelling facts that may have been overlooked by many.

The Hotel Del Coronado is more than just your average seaside resort. Nestled on the white sands of Del, California (just across San Diego Bay), the twenty-eight acre complex is a majestic nod to architecture and design. The hotel was the brainchild of Elisha Babcock, Jr., and Hampton Story. In 1885, the two wealthy entrepreneurs purchased a huge plot of land that encompassed the entire Coronado peninsula. Their dream was to develop the area, compound their initial investments, and build a grand hotel that would attract the world's wealthiest, most influential people.

California was still in its infancy during the latter part of the 19th century, so travelers had limited choices in where to stay; it was necessity over luxury. The Hotel Del Coronado was a welcome option - the ultimate respite for the rich and famous. The construction of the resort was almost completely comprised of native California lumber, including the state's renowned redwood, Douglas fir, cedar, and hemlock. Designers continued the use of fine woods on the interior design of the hotel, including the famous 33 foot high Crown Room ceiling, made of a gorgeous Oregon sugar pine. Known for its sprawling white facade and red tile roof, "The Del" was an unmistakable landmark on the Pacific shores. The "grand Victorian lady" could accommodate up to 1000 visitors with its 400 guestrooms and 71 bathrooms.

The elegance and beauty of the Hotel Del Coronado was designed to attract those of meticulous taste and sophistication. Attention to detail was evident and the entire resort was alive with a sense of luxury. Some of the Del's many amenities catered to guests specific hobbies. Hunting and fishing were a favorite pastime of some of her wealthiest visitors. Guests could bicycle, bowl, and play billiards at their leisure. Quiet areas could be utilized for more passive pursuits such as reading and cards. Technology was also an attractive feature. Electricity and telephones were a novelty in many hotels of the Victorian era, but the Del Coronado had both. Luxuries including private bathrooms and elevators, along with exquisite furnishings and lush decor, helped The Del live up to her divine reputation.

The Pacific ocean frames the hotel in a bright blue border. Layers of soft white sand make the complementary colors pop. The seashore attracts and repels the tides in a gentle but powerful rhythm. It is mesmerizing to beachgoers and those gazing out from the hotel veranda. This was the last view the woman known as Kate Morgan saw before her life ended in flash of gunpowder and smoke.

The legend of "The Beautiful Stranger" began on Thanksgiving day, 1892. A young woman walked in to the lobby of the Hotel Del Coronado, alone. This was significant because, during the Victorian era, it wasn't considered proper for a lady to travel unaccompanied. One would expect a husband, father, or even a brother to chaperone in such instances. Nevertheless, the woman checked in under the name, "Mrs. Lottie A. Bernard." This is the woman we know historically as Kate Morgan. She explained that she was waiting for her brother, Dr. M.C. Anderson, to join her shortly. He was to help her with some sort of medical condition that she never fully divulged. The clerk thought it odd that she carried no luggage or traveling cases.

The unusual woman couldn't help but attract attention. The hotel staff did their best to kept the strange patron happy, but it was clear from the start that things were far from normal. The woman seemed ill. Her doctor brother failed to show, even after several days and numerous inquiries. The hotel management doubted highly that the woman was using her real name or actually waiting for her brother. But she was in desperate need of a physician. She grew weaker and weaker with each passing day, until, by day four, she could barely walk.

Four days after she checked in, the mysterious guest somehow managed the strength to leave the hotel. The staff was completely surprised when the woman, in her frail state, made her way to downtown San Diego. This meant a great deal of walking, followed by a trolley and then a boat ride - and then a return trip back to the hotel. What was so important that she had to make this journey, especially with her compromised health? The answer came quickly. The following day, Lottie Bernard, aka Kate Morgan, was found dead. Her body was discovered on the steps just outside the hotel near the shore, with a fatal gunshot wound to the head. The loaded gun by her side gave authorities the indication that she took her own life. She had apparently gone to San Diego to purchase a gun.

So how does the story of Lottie Bernard become the legend of Kate Morgan? There are so many unanswered questions in this scenario, and so many assumptions that may or may not be true. Author John T. Cullen tackles many of these details in his book, **Dead Move**: **Kate Morgan and the Haunting Mystery of Coronado.** Cullen's interest in the Kate Morgan ghost story was sparked after taking a part-time position as a driver for the Hotel Del Coronado. Cullen was fascinated with the history of the grand hotel and the legend attached to it. Many hotel employees could fluently recite the Kate Morgan story upon request for curious visitors. Cullen was no exception.

But there were things about the story that didn't make sense. Cullen poured through the Del Coronado's account of what happened. The book *"Beautiful Stranger:*

The Ghost of Kate Morgan and the Hotel Del Coronado" is
the official account of the incident. It includes detailed
records and testimonials collected by the Hotel Del
Coronado Heritage Department. Cullen wanted to find
the truth, the motive, or at the very least the true identity
of the mysterious woman known as Kate Morgan.

Lottie A. Bernard was a fictitious name. This is
generally accepted as fact. Kate Morgan was thought to
be her real name. Kate Morgan was indeed a real person,
but was she the woman who checked in to the hotel on
Thanksgiving day in 1892? Who was she waiting for? A
husband? A lover? An unscrupulous doctor who could
provide an alternative to an unwanted pregnancy?
Her's is a tale of love, jealousy, political intrigue,
blackmail, and possibly murder...at least according to
Cullen.

After more than a century, the truth is difficult to
discern. Sources were not always accurate back in the
Victorian era. Newspapers were notorious for printing
salacious, often outrageous stories, written to sell
copies. Facts were not always a priority. This should
be kept in mind when considering print accounts from
that time period, including those who report our story.
What is generally accepted as the truth is this - that
the woman who checked into the Hotel Del Coronado
was NOT Lottie Bernard. But was she, as legend claims,
Kate Morgan? Kate Morgan plays into the story, but not
as the victim. She is quite possibly the instigator of an
incredible tale of blackmail and death.

The real Kate Morgan was a grifter - a con artist,
with a sullied reputation. She had her sights set on
John Spreckels, heir to a fortune in the Hawaiian
Dole pineapple business and owner of the Hotel Del
Coronado. Kate's complicated scheme required a
myriad of players, including one Elizabeth "Lizzie"
Wyllie - a desperate and vulnerable young woman.

Theory suggests that it was Lizzie Wyllie who checked into the Hotel Del Coronado under the pseudonym "Lottie Bernard." Lizzie may have felt she had no other option than to involve herself in the game set forth by Morgan. She had her share of troubles in the past and found herself in a delicate situation. Lizzie had an affair with her married boss, John Longfield, which led to her being fired from her job in Detroit. The affair left her alone, unemployed, and unexpectedly pregnant. Lizzie wanted nothing more than to ensure a future for herself and her child - a child she dearly loved even before it was born.

So how did Lizzie Wyllie (the fictitious Lottie A. Bernard) come to be a pawn in Kate Morgan's confusing and deadly scheme? What was the prime motivation? According to Cullen's research, Kate Morgan wanted to blackmail the hotel's wealthy owner, John Spreckels. Spreckels was engulfed in a political battle to ensure the future of his family's Hawaiian pineapple business at a time when the United States was trying to annex the island nation. The eventual overthrow of the Hawaiian sovereignty is a political tale in its own right. We'll keep it simple, referring only to how Spreckels plays into our story.

Morgan concocted an elaborate con intended to separate Spreckels from a significant portion of his enormous fortune. She needed help, someone whom she could control. The naive and gullible Lizzie Wyllie was the perfect candidate. She was desperate and Morgan knew it. She sent Lizzie (using the name Lottie Bernard) to the Hotel Del Coronado with intentions to contact Spreckels. Bernard would claim to be a secret lover of the powerful businessman, a lover who was now pregnant with his child. Morgan hoped that Spreckels would pay handsomely to make this inconvenient woman go away, thereby keeping his reputation intact.

There were other players in the game and many moving parts. But things didn't go as planned - not for Morgan and certainly not for the woman using the name Lottie Bernard. Before Spreckels could even react to the blackmail scheme, he was rocked with a terrible tragedy at his beloved Hotel Del Coronado. A woman who checked in as Lottie Bernard (our naive Lizzie Wyllie) had died on the grounds from an apparent suicide. The newspapers had a field day with this scandal. This is not what ringleader Kate Morgan had planned. Something happened to Bernard while at the hotel. Maybe she got tired of waiting for the grift to play out. It could be she was stricken ill by a medicine taken to induce a spontaneous miscarriage. She may have been drinking and self-medicating to the point of physical deterioration. Whoever she was waiting for never showed to rescue her from this terrible ordeal. Whatever her secrets, she took them to the grave.

What happened in the days after the death of the mysterious guest of the Hotel Del Coronado are unsettling. Hotel employees told authorities of the strange behavior of guest Lottie Bernard. Her unusual requests and deteriorating physical condition made staff worried as well as puzzled. Staff member Harry West was summoned to room 302 several times over the course of her stay. Sometimes he brought her alcohol that she requested to "ease her pain." She told one employee she had stomach cancer. Around noon on her final day, West had to help the weakened woman dry her hair after she claimed to have fallen in the bathtub.

Hotel Del Coronado's chief clerk, A.S. Gomer told investigators that Lottie Bernard inquired several times about any messages from her "brother." He doubted the man she was waiting for was actually her brother at all. She said that he had the claim checks to her luggage from the train, which would explain her checking in without bags. Gomer was more concerned with her hotel bill, which was growing day by day. Bernard told him that a man named G.L. Allen in Hamburg, Iowa would cover her with a line of credit. Indeed, a Hamburg bank sent $25 to the Hotel Del Coronado for the expenses of "Lottie A. Bernard." The money arrived shortly after her body was found.

The mysterious brother was now thought to be her lover. According to Cullen's theory, Lottie Bernard was actually Lizzie Wyllie, who was waiting for her married lover, John Longfield, to join her in California. Kate Morgan may have assured the pregnant and unwed girl that arrangements were made for Longfield to join her. She just had to play her part and go along with the Spreckles blackmail scheme. The couple would be rewarded handsomely for the ruse - enough money to ensure a good life for themselves and their future child. Lizzie, in her weakened state, may have changed her mind. She would no longer be involved in the plan that Kate Morgan had talked her into. She only wanted to be reunited with her lover and be a mother to her unborn baby. But something went terribly wrong. She lost all hope. Faced with a life of loneliness and shame, the poor girl committed suicide.

The inquiry into the incident was handled poorly. A preliminary autopsy was rushed and the police seemed eager to wrap up what little investigation was done. It became clear to many that the woman in question was not named Lottie Bernard. One hotel guest claimed to have witnessed an argument on a train between a woman fitting her description and an unknown man. The man stormed, off leaving the woman distraught and alone. Could this be the same woman who checked in without luggage at the Del? Who was she and what was she here for?

Investigators at that time believed Lottie Bernard

was actually a woman named Kate (or Katie) Morgan, a domestic servant from Los Angeles. She had traveled to the Hotel Del Coronado for the holiday, leaving her job as a housekeeper for a few days of relaxation and fun. Belongings left at her job tied her to the woman at the Del. One piece of evidence that connects her to the story is the money used to pay the hotel bill. The funds came from Hamburg, Iowa - Kate Morgan's hometown. There were other possible "Kate Morgans" that came up during an investigation, none that could be irrefutably tied to the dead woman at the Hotel Del Coronado.

Cullen found many holes in the story that just didn't add up. There were even wild theories that the mysterious hotel guest did not commit suicide; she was murdered. Much of the physical evidence was washed away by the storm. Interesting, but unlikely. Why was the entire investigation so rushed and mishandled? Could it be that John Spreckels wanted the whole thing to go away? Maybe he was aware of Morgan's intentions to blackmail him. Who actually wired the line of credit to the hotel? Who was the doctor/brother who never showed? Where was the luggage?

The newspaper accounts of the incident follow along a rocky path of speculation and inconsistencies. An autopsy revealed that the dead woman found near the back steps of the Hotel Del Coronado was pregnant. This hinted at a reason for her suicide. Authorities seemed to be in agreement that she was not Lottie A Bernard. The death certificate (which was lost and reissued at least once) read "Lottie A. Bernard, aka Kate Morgan" and had the wrong date listed for her death. Innocent mistakes? Possibly. Or maybe evidence of a cover-up. It is possible, according to Cullen, that John Spreckels got wind of the planned blackmail attempt by Morgan and put in motion his own scheme to keep his name out of the limelight.

On the surface it's a sad story of a distraught woman. But when you look deeper, the lines between truth and deception begin to blur. Fingers point in all directions. The puzzle pieces don't fit together neatly, instead there are holes and glaring discrepancies. One thing remains clear. The woman who checked in the Hotel Del Coronado on that Thanksgiving day was dead. Her erratic behavior and mounting physical decline was apparent to everyone she encountered during her brief stay. Her sadness and despair were palpable.

Was she there to blackmail the wealthy John Spreckels? Was she Lizzie Wyllie, waiting for her married lover to join her so they could live happily ever after? Did she come to have an abortion, the only choice she thought she had after becoming pregnant by a married man? Was she the domestic servant from Los Angeles, Kate Morgan, or was she the known grifter from Iowa with the same name?

The mystery may never be solved to the satisfaction of those who've researched the story extensively. Officially, the Beautiful Stranger of the Hotel Del Coronado is Kate Morgan. She may have been a jilted lover, or just a sick and lonely woman with little hope. John T Cullen believes he has solved the mystery and identified the Beautiful Stranger as the naive and desperate Lizzie Wyllie. She was in a delicate state when the devious con artist Kate Morgan got hold of her and convinced her to take part in a poorly thought out blackmail scheme.

Regardless of where the truth lies, there is one thing we know for sure - The Hotel Del Coronado is haunted. A beautiful but sullen apparition of a woman has been spotted numerous times gracefully gliding across the sandy sea shore. The ethereal entity fades into the mist like the outgoing fog at twilight. The same mysterious figure haunts the meticulously maintained halls of the hotel, favoring the room where Kate Morgan is said to have stayed. Sometimes guests hear a faint cry coming

44

from the balcony of their suite. Others report a strange woman watching them as they sleep. Objects move by themselves and small items mysteriously disappear, only to reappear later. The water in certain guest rooms likes to turn on and off by itself.

The paranormal activity at the Hotel Del Coronado seems to revolve around our ghost Kate, but she is not alone. The spirit of another woman, a housekeeper, is said to haunt the guest rooms of the beautiful resort. Rumors say she was pregnant when she took her own life. Maybe it is the similarity in circumstance that keeps her on our earthly plane. There have also been reports of two children that run the halls at night, giggling happily. They've been spotted peering out of windows of unoccupied rooms. Staff investigate to see if maybe some guest's mischievous youngsters have managed to sneak into these rooms by themselves. But they find only locked doors and silence. These ghostly youngsters are more playful than frightening, yet no one knows where they came from.

It seems the Del has had quite a few unregistered guests staying with them over the years. The ghost known as Kate Morgan wanders the hotel where she spent her last few agonizing days. Records show that numerous visitors assigned to room 3327 (the new number of Kate's original room) have urgently insisted on moving in the middle of the night, claiming the room was already occupied...by a spirit! Kate Morgan roams both inside the Del and outside, especially near the place where she took her own life. Maybe the calming movement of the waves draws her to the water's edge, giving solace to her tortured soul.

The Beautiful Stranger, the Hotel Del Coronado's longest resident guest, remains alone in the afterlife, still waiting for someone or something. Maybe she will haunt the area until her identity is confirmed, until we know with certainty who she was and why she came to San Diego Bay. I believe, as John T Cullen does, that the poor woman they call Kate Morgan is actually Lizzie Wyllie - an unfortunate young girl in a delicate state. She was lured to the hotel with the promise of a better life. She wanted only to be with the man she so desperately loved and be a mother to the baby growing inside her belly. The Beautiful Stranger's only crime was love. Now, more than a century after her death, she seeks forgiveness and peace.

LOVE BETRAYED

Grace Brown And Chester Gillette

O nce in a while, the elements in a story line up perfectly with all the components needed for a haunting tale of passion and betrayal. A scandalous romance, intrigue, murder, followed by a ghost. This is one of those perfect haunted love stories.

Collecting eggs from the chickens, milking the cows, weeding the garden, helping her mother take care of her seven brothers and sisters...this was the life of Grace Brown. In the late nineteenth century, Grace lived on a farm in South Otselic, located in Upstate New York. She attended the nearby Tallett school. In a sense, life seemed somewhat idyllic for this rural area. There was a village center with a post office, general store, and a variety of businesses supplying the essential needs of this small community.

Living in Otselic was quite comfortable. Grace's home was located in a remote area where dairy farms dotted the bucolic landscape. This farming community was surrounded by verdigris hills that rose above the fertile valleys. Small streams were plentiful. Farmhouses were separated by acres of rolling pastures. In 1904, the life of a simple country girl did not hold promise for Grace, nicknamed "Billy" because of her love for the song, **Won't You Come Home Bill Bailey**. The drudgery of farm life made her long for more exciting things that might be found in the city. Her older sister, Ada, had married and moved to Courtland, which was thirty-one miles east of South Otselic. Ada wrote letters to Grace about the many experiences of living in the city. Grace was intrigued by the letters and made the decision it was time to leave her safe and predictable life in the little hamlet of South Otselic.

Great economic growth had begun as the textile industry changed to automation, and many jobs were readily available to rural daughters. Grace, the young and attractive country girl, decided she needed to make her move and become a city girl.

Bidding her family goodbye, she made the journey to live with her sister and brother-in-law. She sought employment at the successful Gillette Skirt Factory located in Courtland. Grace was immediately hired and began working as a fabric cutter for a small but fair wage.

Noah Gillette, the owner of the Skirt Factory, was a wealthy businessman. He held patents on corsets and other wardrobe essentials that made him a very prosperous individual. His company was thriving. He decided to mentor his young nephew, Chester, in the family business. Chester Gillette withdrew from the prestigious Oberlin College of Ohio to work for his uncle. He arrived in Courtland in 1905 and began working in the stockroom.

The young Grace Brown, a pretty girl with dark brown hair, hazel eyes, and a fetching figure, met the extremely handsome Chester Gillette at the Skirt Factory in the Spring of 1905. They quickly became friends and were seen in each other's company very regularly at work.

Love Betrayed

Before long the two became linked romantically, at the considerable disapproval of Grace's friends. They felt Chester's high society ways and constant womanizing were not going to lead the romance in the proper direction. In fact, he did not even acknowledge the close relationship while they were at work. Despite opposition, the two soon became lovers.

Chester would visit Grace frequently at her sister Ada's house and was welcomed as a proper suitor by the family. However, it turns out their relationship was exclusively sexual in nature, at least on the part of Chester. About twice a week Chester would arrive at Grace's for their clandestine dalliances. They were never seen out in public on a proper date. Conjecture on where their relationship was headed was often the main topic of conversation by the gossips at work.

Ada and her husband Clarence decided it was time to relocate, and Grace found herself without a place to stay. After taking some time to weigh her options, she made the courageous decision to stay in Courtland. We can speculate her main motivation was to be near Chester. Grace found a boarding house near the factory and moved in. Her landlady was very congenial.

Grace had many close friends among her co-workers and she felt fulfilled at work. However, her main concern was her relationship with Chester. As with most women looking for commitment, she longed for a proper courtship and romance that was more than just a sexual affair. Knowing her virtue was no longer intact and her reputation sullied, she anticipated that eventually, Chester would put a ring on her finger.

Then the unimaginable happened. In the spring of 1906, Grace Brown discovered she was pregnant. This could mean ruin for a young unmarried woman. When she gave her lover the news, Chester began to distance himself from her. He started attending more of the high

49

society parties to which he was frequently invited. It was said Chester was keeping close company with a particular woman who ran in his same social circle. His indiscretions were pointed out to Grace by her friends, and his duplicitous attitude was evident. She became frightened, thinking Chester did not intend to do the honorable thing and marry her.

Grace became more and more emboldened in her desperation as she expressed these concerns to Chester. It seemed he would err on the side of caution and not push her away, even after she threatened to tell everyone. He knew this could ruin his family name and he did not wish to experience the wrath of his uncle. Chester advised Grace that she should go home to South Otselic and spend some time with her family. This way he could have time to think and formulate a strategy. He even asked her if she would consider having an abortion. After an emphatic "no," Grace left for her parent's home.

While at home with her family, Grace imagined Chester was planning for them to run away. She spent her days sewing an extensive trousseau for their anticipated secret wedding. Or so she presumed. When there was no communication from Chester, Grace began to worry. She wrote to him each day, with themes of undying devotion, while also communicating the anguish she felt from suspicions of unrequited love.

She expressed great heartache over leaving her family permanently. During several of these poignant missives, she went as far as to mention she would be better off dead than in her current predicament. Chester wrote to her once or twice. His message left his intentions up in the air and basically encouraged her to sit tight and wait because he was devising a plan. There were several times he wrote he would meet her on a particular date and time, but he never showed. Something always came up. He had endless excuses as to why he suddenly could not keep the dates.

After more than three weeks, Chester contacted Grace, asking her to meet him in DeRuyter on July 9. From there they would take the train to the Upper New York region and the Adirondack Mountains where they could spend time together. At this point, Grace may have assumed Chester was going to propose, even suspecting they may get married while on this trip. It is known that she packed her entire wardrobe in a trunk to take on the journey. Grace made arrangements for transportation to DeRuyter by hiring a wagon. She made it to the station just in time to jump on the departing train. This was the beginning of the trip that would prove to be fatal.

After Grace reunited with Chester, they took the train and spent their first night in the Hotel Martin in Utica, New York. While registering for their stay, Chester used a fictitious name, making sure the initials matched his monogrammed luggage. He gave the title "Charles Gordon and wife." The next day their train arrived at Tupper Lake. Again, while checking in to the local hotel, assumed names were used. They continued their journey upstate, arriving on the shores of the picturesque Big Moose Lake for a stay at the Glenmore Hotel. Once again, Chester registered under a pseudonym. But this time the registry bore Grace's true Identity.

Chester checked in with one suitcase, a tennis racket, and a camera. Grace had high hopes that this was the day of her elopement ceremony, and the time she would begin her new life as Mrs. Chester Gillette. Unfortunately, her trunk had remained on the train and gone through to the next town. Soon after they checked into their room, the couple traveled down to the lake side. Chester rented a small rowboat for a sightseeing tour of Big Moose Lake. It was the 11th of July.

As they pushed their boat off the shore, Chester and Grace appeared to be any other young couple going for a row out on the water. In an unusual twist, Chester had taken his suitcase, camera, and tennis racket with him onto the boat. They drifted farther and farther onto the glassy lake, soon out of view of those on the shoreline. They explored all the inlets and even pulled up on a remote shore for a brief rest. Others out on the lake reported seeing them that day.

Later that evening, the proprietor of the boat rental operation became concerned when the rented skiff had not returned. By twilight, he made a cursory search for the couple. Not being able to find them or the rowboat in the dark, he decided to try again in the morning. Less than twenty-four hours later, Grace's lifeless and beaten body was recoered from an isolated cove on the lake, submerged in about eight feet of water. The overturned rowboat was floating nearby. There was no sign of Chester Gillette. A manhunt for the suspected killer was organized by local authorities. After two days of searching, Gillette was found attending a party at a nearby hotel, carrying on as if he hadn't a care in the world.

It seemed the pregnant Grace Brown thought a romantic row around the lake was a precursor to a proposal. But it wasn't marriage that Chester Gillette had in mind - it was murder. Filled with anticipation, Grace stifled her excitement and tried to enjoy the beauty and calmness of the lake. Without warning, the serene silence was broken by a loud thwack! It was the sound of Chester's tennis racket as it violently struck the side of her head. The force of the blow sent her over the side of the boat and into the deadly water. And poor Grace could not swim, which was a fact Chester knew. An autopsy revealed bruising on her forehead and cheeks. Her lips were cut, swollen, and discolored.

There was a deep laceration on Grace's head which the coroner speculated was responsible for rendering her unconscious. It was suggested that the murder weapon was Chester Gillette's tennis racket.

Gillette was arrested and charged with the murder of Grace Brown. He was incarcerated in Herkimer County jail until November. The prosecutor was ready to go the distance and send this killer to his execution. The press gathered their many sources and provided the public with an abundance of information. The nation watched in morbid fascination as the gruesome details of the crime came to light. The murder of Grace Brown was more than news, it was journalistic sensationalism. Chester Gillette was tried and convicted in the minds of the public before his litigation even began.

The prosecution compiled an extensive amount of evidence against Chester. For some unknown reason, Chester had saved most of Grace's love letters which the police recovered when they searched his room. They were entered as evidence and read in open court. At one point, District Attorney George Ward read a heartbreaking segment from one of Grace's letters:

> *I am so blue. Oh dear, if you were only here and would kiss me and tell me not to worry any more... I will try so hard to please you. Darling, if you will only write and tell me that you will surely come Saturday and not to worry. I am crying so I can't see the lines... You will never know, dear, how badly I feel or how much I want you this minute.*

Newspapers reported that during the readings of Grace's anguished letters there was not a dry eye in the courtroom, except for the eyes of Chester Gillette. He was called a "callous, cold-hearted brute." The police feared the intense public scrutiny and ensuing outcry.

The word on the street was that people were planning to storm the jail and bring Gillette out themselves to lynch him on the public square!

During the trial, several gruesome aspects of the murder were presented in the open courtroom. The doctor who examined Grace's body was called as a witness. At one point the District Attorney calmly walked across the courtroom carrying a large jar. The doctor was asked what was in the jar. The physician claimed it contained a uterus and a dead fetus. When asked to whom they belonged, the doctor explained they were removed from the body of Grace Brown during the autopsy.

Chester Gillette took the stand in his own defense and offered the least plausible of accounts of what happened that warm July day on Big Moose Lake. He claimed that he urged Grace to go to her father and confess the whole story. He went on to explain that at this point Grace became so distraught with his suggestion that she jumped into the lake and drowned herself. When asked why he didn't reach out to save her, Gillette had no answer.

Of course, the jury didn't believe his story. After a three-week trial, he was convicted of murder in the first degree. The judge sentenced Chester Gillette to death and sent him to Auburn Prison. In March of 1908, he was executed in the electric chair for the murder of Grace Brown.

Soon after the execution, prisoners who found themselves confined to the cell previously occupied by Gillette complained that someone or something was in the cell with them. They claimed they were awakened at night by the vision of Chester Gillette standing by the side of their cot. Many prisoners begged to be relocated. Screams in the night coming from the cell became so common that the sheriff issued an order that this particular cell would remain vacant, only to be used in the case of a full prison.

These ghostly reports have continued through the years. The Herkimer County Jail is still in existence today. Also standing is the courthouse, which is currently the headquarters for the Herkimer County Sheriff's Department. Tours of the area can be arranged through the Herkimer County Historical Society.

Many continue to be fascinated by the story of Grace Brown and Chester Gillette. The tale went on to inspire a number of plays, songs, books, and movies. The 1925 novel, "An American Tragedy" authored by Theodore Dreiser, was based on the tragic events. That book went on to influence the award-winning 1951 movie, "A Place in the Sun," starring Elizabeth Taylor, Shelly Winters, and Montgomery Clift.

Numerous sightings of the ghost of Grace Brown are reported from the area around Big Moose Lake. On misty nights, an apparition of a skiff can be seen. At first, the skiff appears to be abandoned. It seems to float slowly towards those watching from the shoreline. Suddenly, a phantom woman materializes, falling from the boat into the water. The scene vanishes as quickly as it appears. Her ghost is also seen walking slowly along the lakeshore. Several people who have stayed at the rental cottages along the lake report visits from Grace's specter. They say she has a tendency to extinguish all the lights unexpectedly.

A female vacationer reported an interesting encounter with Grace's ghost. During an evening walk from the cabin to the shoreline, she felt as if she were being watched from the surrounding woods. She even heard footsteps following closely behind her on the path. As the tourist approached the lake, her flashlight shut off. She became frightened and turned around to head back to the cabin. Suddenly, she was confronted by an ethereal woman blocking her way. As she screamed, the apparition mysteriously vanished.

Even those who stay at the family home in South Otselic, New York, have reported that the phantom of Grace Brown lingers there. People who have spent time in the house describe close encounters with her ghost. They recount being awakened in the early hours of the night by footsteps on the stairs, unusual creaking, and noises outside their bedroom door. The banging and rattling of pots and pans echo from the kitchen when no one is there.

The story concludes with a tragic ending. Is it any surprise that the ghost of Grace Brown wishes to be remembered at a place filled with youthful innocence and tranquility before a killer ended her life?

DEVOTED LOVE

Zona Heaster Shue, The Greenbrier Ghost

There is no greater love than that of mother and child. A mother's love can move mountains and accomplish impossible feats of strength. A mother instinctively knows when her child is hurt or in pain. There is nothing she wouldn't do for her child. This maternal bond can never be broken, even in death.

Never was there a more perfect example of this than in the case of Mary Jane Heaster and her beloved daughter, Zona.

Zona's untimely death could not sever the connection between the two women, despite the physical and even legal limitations they encountered. Tethered by love, and fueled by loss, rage, and the need to expose a terrible injustice - Mary Jane and Zona made history.

This is the strange tale of the Greenbrier Ghost - the spirit that solved her own murder. This was the first (and only) time that testimony from a ghost was admitted as evidence in a United States Superior Court trial. This was a legal recognition of the supernatural - a supernatural declaration from beyond the grave. It was a landmark case in American history.

There are many theories as to why ghosts exist. Some are more palpable than others. Trapped souls, a tortured conscience, spirits lost and confused wandering aimlessly in the ether. Maybe they don't realize they're dead, or they fear the consequences that await them on the other side. One popular viewpoint is that sometimes a ghost remains on this earthly plane because of unfinished business. There is some important task that must be done before the deceased can truly rest in peace. In the case of Elva Zona Heaster Shue (known as Zona), that business was justice.

Nothing much ever happened in the sleepy town of Meadow Bluff. It was a picturesque community tucked away in Greenbrier County, West Virginia. This was where Mary Jane Heaster raised her daughter, Zona, and dreamed of future grandchildren.

Zona never strayed far from her birthplace, even after she married Erasmus, aka "Trout," Stribbling Shue. He was a physically strong man, several years senior to Zona. He was said to be "old fashioned" in his beliefs when it came to women and marriage. He expected a subservient wife and tried to mold Zona into his ideal. The couple made Lewisburg, in Greenbrier, their home. Zona was happy to remain close to her mother. They were more than just mother and daughter; they were the best of friends.

Zona and Trout's three-month marriage was not the fairytale union a young girl dreams about. Trout was controlling, quick to anger, and sometimes violent. Zona found herself desperately trying to please her husband but falling short of his lofty expectations. Tensions in the Shue home were high. Mary Jane constantly worried about her daughter, who, despite the problems, wanted desperately to make her marriage work.

On the morning of January 23, 1897, a young neighbor boy named Andy was sent to the home of Trout and

Zona Shue to collect eggs. He often did chores for the couple while Trout was away at work. When Andy arrived, he was met with an empty chicken coop and an eerie silence.

Young Andy knocked on the door of the Shue home but got no answer. He called out but there was no response. Mrs. Shue was expecting him, so he thought it strange the house was so quiet. Slowly, he announced himself and pushed open the unlocked door. He was met with a grisly sight. There, on the floor was the body of 23-year-old Zona. She was face down, her body outstretched in an unnatural manner and her neck slightly askew. It was evident that she was dead.

The startled boy dropped his basket and ran to fetch his mother, screaming at the top of his lungs that Mrs. Shue was dead. The two rushed to the blacksmith shop where Trout was working and told him about the gruesome discovery. The frantic announcement was like a kick in the gut. Trout dropped his tools and hurried back to the house. There he found his young bride lying lifeless on the floor. Witnesses said Trout was hysterical.

Local physician, Dr. George Knapp was called to examine the corpse and officially pronounced Zona Heaster Shue dead. He searched for clues as to why the healthy young woman had suddenly died. He also thought it odd that the body had already been moved, cleaned, and dressed by Trout. For the sake of modesty, it was customary for women to handle the delicate details in such circumstances.

With the distraught husband continually hovering above him, Dr. Knapp began a cursory examination of the body. He tried to unfasten the high collar on Zona's dress. Before he got a good look at the back of the neck, Trout intervened and insisted he stop. He angrily demanded that his wife's body not be disturbed anymore. The frustrated doctor stopped the examination and left the house. Dr. Knapp chalked up Shue's odd behavior to the shock of losing his wife.

The official cause of death was an "everlasting faint," another way of saying Zona's heart mysteriously stopped. Dr. Knapp found nothing unusual to explain the young woman's sudden collapse. He concluded that she simply died of natural causes. But not all in Greenbrier were so easily convinced.

The following day, a wake was held at Zona's mother's house. During the service, the attendees noticed more odd behavior from Trout. Beyond what one would expect from a grieving husband, Trout was fully immersed in a show of sorrow and despair. He stayed close to the body, sobbing inconsolably as he cradled Zona's head in his arms. He physically deterred mourners from getting too close.

Trout was fidgety, constantly adjusting Zona's body. He put a pillow under her head and tied a scarf around her neck. He tearfully claimed it was his wife's favorite. He exhibited a rather exaggerated show of emotions; crying and wailing like a man in unbearable emotional pain. Mary Jane Heaster, although tear filled and heartbroken herself, was suspicious of Trout's "grieving husband" performance. Call it women's intuition or motherly instinct, she knew something wasn't right.

Trout buried Zona Heaster Shue in the Soul Chapel Methodist Cemetery in Greenbrier County, West Virginia. The community mourned the loss of a beautiful young woman, taken too soon from this earthly plane. But Zona would not rest in peace. Her anguished spirit turned to the one person who could help - her mother.

Mary Jane Heaster didn't accept that her healthy young daughter could suddenly drop dead. She believed it must have been something far more sinister. She also heard some unsettling rumors about her son-in-law that called into question his character and his past. Being a good Christian woman, she prayed for answers. Every night for four weeks Mary Jane prayed. And her prayers were answered in a most unusual way.

For four consecutive nights, Mary Jane was visited by the ghost of her beloved daughter. The apparition was peculiar, even from a supernatural standpoint. At first, it appeared as a spectacular white light. The light pulsated and grew brighter, finally morphing into a familiar female form.

Standing before her, emanating from the brilliant white radiance, was her daughter, back from the dead. It was neither a dream nor a hallucination. An ethereal glow surrounded Zona as she approached her startled mother. Zona was there, corporeal, in the flesh, as solid as she was in life, wearing the dress she had on the day she died. She reached for her mother with a terrible longing in her eyes. Mary Jane was fully awake and aware when the visitations occurred. This was not a manifestation of her grief.

During these bizarre events, Zona communicated with her mother, talking about her life and short but tumultuous relationship with Trout. Zona shared vivid details about her home and her marriage. She clearly articulated events that led up to her death. Zona was distraught, her spirit unable to rest until someone knew the truth. She reached out from beyond the grave pleading for justice.

Zona made proclamations that sent shivers down her mother's spine. She had been the victim of a terrible crime. Zona's life with Trout was not a pleasant one. He was a violent man with a short temper, and she always got the worst of it. On that fateful January morning, Trout Shue, angry there was no meat for dinner, went on a violent rampage. The frightened Zona pleaded with him and desperately tried to calm him down. Her efforts were met with a savage physical attack. In a fit of rage, Trout grabbed his frail frightened wife by her neck. Gasping for air and terrified, she begged him to stop. Zona's cries were muffled by her husband's angry guttural groans. Trout pressed his calloused hands around her delicate throat and squeezed until he felt the life force leave her body.

Mary Jane was dumbfounded. Her worst fears were realized. She knew the sudden passing of her daughter was not an unavoidable tragedy - it was a horrific act of fury. Each time Zona appeared, she revealed more and more information about the day she died. Zona could never rest in peace until people knew the truth about her murderous husband.

Mary Jane Heaster was desperate and determined to help her daughter. She contacted authorities demanding that Zona's body be exhumed and examined properly. She didn't care about the resistance or opposition she'd face with such a request. She was fighting for her daughter's soul.

Mary Jane somehow convinced the local prosecutor, John Preston, to listen to her incredible and implausible story. Preston found her so convincing that he agreed to take another look at the case. To his surprise, he uncovered some previously undisclosed and alarming information about Trout. Trout Shue spent time in prison for assault and theft. He had also been married twice before he met Zona. Preston discovered one of Trout's two previous wives had also died under "mysterious circumstances."

As if this wasn't damning enough, Trout Shue was heard running his mouth about how no one could ever prove he killed his wife. On February 22, 1897, Zona's body was brought back to the coroner's office for a proper postmortem examination. Drs. Knapp, Rupert, and McClung conducted the examination of the body.

To their surprise, they found visible physical evidence of foul play. The neck was dislocated between the first and second vertebrae. The ligaments were torn and ruptured. They also found bruising that resembled fingers on her throat.

The doctors agreed that Zona's windpipe had been crushed. The official cause of death was "anoxia from manual strangulation compounded by a broken neck." No other injuries were noted on the body. Zona had not died of an everlasting faint. She was murdered.

The damning evidence pointed to the grieving widower, Trout Shue. Zona's spirit guided her mother to the truth of exactly what happened that January morning. Trout was immediately arrested and charged with murder. He was seemingly unaffected by the trial. Although he had no alibi for the morning of his wife's death, he knew there was no witness, no one who saw his deadly deed. How could a dead woman point a finger at him?

On June 22, 1897, the most spectacular murder trial in West Virginia history began. The State of West Virginia vs. Erasmus (Edward) Stribbling Shue. The accused was brought before a judge and jury of his peers to answer to the charges. Even with the physical evidence found on Zona's body, the prosecution still had an uphill battle. How could Preston convince the jury that it was a ghost that cracked the case?

The people of Greenbrier County bore witness to the trial of the century. This was an unprecedented murder case, unlike anything they had seen before. Mary Jane Heaster was the star witness for the state. Her tale was incredible. The testimony she gave was word-for-word what her dead daughter's ghost told her.

The defense's only hope was to attack Mary Jane's credibility, call into question her very sanity. They tried to convince the jury that the distraught mother was dreaming or hallucinating. Instead, they heard Mary Jane describe in graphic detail the four visitations from Zona. She remained steadfast that she hadn't dreamed the events. She was not a superstitious wacko or a woman delusional with grief.

The following is an excerpt from the actual court testimony of Mary Jane Heaster regarding the visits from her dead daughter. Council for the defense questioned the prosecution's star witness, Mary Jane Heaster.

Q. Now, Mrs. Heaster, this sad affair was very particularly impressed upon your mind, and there was not a moment during your waking hours that you did not dwell upon it?

A. No, sir; and there is not yet, either.

Q. And this was not a dream founded upon your distressed condition of mind?

A. No, sir. It was no dream, for I was as awake as I ever was.

Q. Then if not a dream or dreams, what do you call it?

A. I prayed to the Lord that she might come back and tell me what happened, and I prayed that she might come herself and tell on him.

Q. Do you think you actually saw her in flesh and blood?

A. Yes, sir, I do. I told them the very dress that she was killed in, and when she went to leave me she turned her head completely around and looked at me like she wanted me to know all about it. And the very next time she came back to me she told me all about it. The first time she came, she *seemed that she did not want to tell me as much about it as she did afterwards. The last night she was there she told me that she did everything she could do, and I am satisfied that she did do all that, too.*

Q. Now, Mrs. Heaster, don't you know that these visions, as you term them or describe them, were nothing more or less than four dreams founded upon your distress?

A. No, I don't know it. The Lord sent her to me to tell it. I was the only friend that she knew she could tell and put any confidence it; I was the nearest one to her. He gave me a ring that he pretended she wanted me to have, but I don't know what dead woman he might have taken it off of. I wanted her own ring and he would not let me have it.

Q. Mrs. Heaster, are you positively sure that these are not four Dreams?

A. Yes, sir. It was not a dream. I don't dream when I am wide awake, to be sure; and I know I saw her right there with me.

Mary Jane was unshakable on the witness stand. She spoke with confidence and urgency. She had to bring a malicious murderer to justice so her daughter could finally rest in peace. The bizarre story was the most unusual testimony ever given in a West Virginia court.

As for Trout, he arrogantly took the stand and declared his innocence. He alleged that he loved his wife and her death was an unforeseeable tragedy. He claimed to be the victim of a hateful attack by his jealous, delusional mother-in-law. He pleaded with the court to dismiss the outrageous charges against him. The jury didn't believe the "grieving husband" act.

Unable to turn Mary Jane's testimony, the defense rested, as did the prosecution. The strength of her convictions carried her through the hardships of the trial and the relentless attacks on her character. The judge made a final statement before sending the jury off to deliberate. They were given the following instructions:

> "There was no living witness to the crime charged against Defendant Shue and the State rests its case for conviction wholly upon circumstances connecting the accused with the murder charged. So, the connection of the accused with the crime depends entirely upon the strength of the circumstantial evidence introduced by the State. There is no middle ground for you, the jury, to take. The verdict inevitably and logically must be for murder in the first degree or for an acquittal."

With those words fresh in their minds, the jury deliberated. It was all or nothing for conviction or exoneration. Would they concur with the idea that an unjustly murdered wife could return from beyond the grave and point an accusing finger at her abusive husband?

In just over an hour, they came back with a verdict - GUILTY!

In an unprecedented legal proceeding, the testimony of a ghost was accepted as evidence. In the landmark case of the State vs. E.S. Shue, a grieving mother, a trio of doctors, and the restless ghost of a slain woman came together to put a murderer behind bars. It was justice served from beyond the grave.

Zona Heaster Shue is known throughout West Virginia and the United States as the Greenbrier Ghost. She sought not to terrify but to expose a horrific crime.

66

If not for the powerful and unbreakable bond of love between mother and child, her death may have never been avenged.

Theresa Argie & Cathi Weber

LOVE LOST

Willie And Nellie Gordon

Many families have stories and legends that are passed down from generation to generation. These ancestral tales reflect the history of our descendants, kept alive through preserved documents, personal letters or even a tradition of oral storytelling. But how many families can boast a well-documented ghost story among their collected anecdotes?

Juliette Gordon Low, the founder of the Girl Scouts of America (1912), is part of a family with a compelling ghost story to share. The home in Savannah, Georgia, where she was born, is the setting of this haunted tale. And Juliette's parents, Willie and Nellie Gordon, are our loving spectral subjects.

The Wayne-Gordon home, a national historic landmark is known as "The Birthplace." In deference to Juliette Gordon Low, it is visited daily by scores of Girl Scouts on pilgrimage to their founder's home. This museum is a central figure for tourism in Savannah. Built in 1821, the large pink stucco mansion, constructed in the architectural style of a regency townhouse, is located on the corner of Bull and Ogelthorpe. The home brings to life the fascinating history of a family that helped shape what would become the future of Savannah.

William Washington Gordon II, nicknamed Willie, was born in 1834. He was the son of W.W. Gordon I, builder of the Central Railroad of Georgia. This railroad, funded by Willie's father, connected Charleston, NC with Savannah, GA. It was integral to the economic growth and success of the state of Georgia. Willie grew up in the mansion, and was groomed from his birth to aid with the Gordon's cotton business. The system of agriculture required to maintain a cotton plantation relied on slave labor. Holding slaves was a common practice and part of the lifestyle Willie was accustomed to in the Deep South.

Eleanor Lytle Kinzie, nicknamed Nellie, was born in Chicago, Illinois in 1835. Her family was of pioneer stock. An ancestral home belonging to her grandfather, John Kinzie, was the first built in what became Chicago. John was well known among the tribes of Indians in that region as a peaceful man and a trustworthy trader. Her grandmother, Margaret, also recorded many interactions with Native-Americans while settling in the Northwest territory. Many credit the Kinzie family as being among the first people to permanently settle in Chicago. Their granddaughter Nellie was a high-spirited girl, raised by cultivated parents in what was thought of as the wilderness.

But how could Willie, a genteel southern gentleman, and Nellie, an animated free-thinking northern girl, meet and fall in love? It appears their backgrounds might present a few challenges! Nellie and Eliza Gordon, the sister of Willie, both attended the prestigious Madame Canda's Boarding School in New York. They were roommates and close friends. Willie attended Yale University in New Haven, Connecticut. Nellie and Eliza would often visit New Haven to stay with friends during school breaks. On one such visit to New Haven, Eliza made plans to visit her brother at Yale. She was excited to introduce Nellie and Willie. They agreed they would meet in the college library.

Nellie and Willie's formal introduction became quite the event to remember. The carefree Nellie had a habit of sliding down banisters instead of walking down the stairs, feeling it was quicker and more efficient. She proceeded to slide down the library banister from the second floor, landing squarely on top of Willie. In the process she ruined his new hat. You could say she left a lasting impression on the young man. Their unique introduction along with Nellie's effervescent personality attracted Willie immediately. They quickly became friends and their relationship blossomed. It's said Nellie kept her vivacious ways, as well as her habit of banister sliding, almost until her death.

The chemistry between the two was undeniable. Willie and Nellie fell deeply in love. They wed in 1857. Willie brought his new bride to live in his grand Savannah home, which he shared with his mother. Their marriage appears to have held true to the old adage that opposites attract. Nellie, being a "Yankee" from Chicago, was a strict abolitionist. Willie was a staunch supporter of slavery and was president of the Savannah Cotton Exchange for many years.

Nellie respected Willie's deep-seated traditions while continuing to maintain her own rooted principles. She was from a family who founded the Episcopal Church in Chicago but Willie was Presbyterian from birth. Nellie persuaded Willie to give up his Presbyterian upbringing and join the Episcopal Church.

Nellie was known for her extremely stubborn will and liberal use of profanity. She was even considered a tomboy. Willie appeared a genteel fellow who followed the strict code of the southern gentleman. He was introspective and reserved. She was boisterous and outgoing. And yet, love found a way. The bond they shared was forged through time never to be broken - even after death.

The life the Gordons lived in Savannah was quite comfortable, even through the turbulent years of the Civil War. They began to grow their family and Nellie gave birth in 1858 to their first daughter, Eleanor. Next came Juliette in 1860. By 1872, with the addition of a daughter and two sons, their family was complete.

The Gordons experienced endless turmoil and conflict throughout the years of the "War between the States." William Gordon was in service to the Georgia Hussars, a group of volunteers from the south who formed a cavalry troop to fight alongside the Confederate forces. Nellie's brother, John, died while in service to the Union during the war, and two of her remaining brothers were captured by Confederate forces.

Nellie Gordon was a very outspoken and persuasive woman. She convinced both Union General W.T. Sherman and Confederate General Robert E. Lee to aid in the search for her husband at different times during the war. First, she went to Virginia with an escort appointed by General Lee. After Willie and Nellie were reunited, she rushed back to Savannah to hide the family valuables before Federal forces arrived in her city.

When Union armies captured Savannah, General Sherman paid a personal visit to Nellie to check on her welfare. He brought mail from her family, gifts for the children, and even had a band play for their enjoyment. When Confederate officer's wives were asked to leave the city after the siege, General Sherman provided an escort for Nellie. This allowed her to travel to South Carolina and say goodbye to her husband before fleeing with her family to the North. After the war, General Gordon returned safely home to Savannah.

William Gordon would be called into service once again with the Hussars when he was commissioned as a brigadier general during the Spanish American War in 1898. His command post was at Camp Miami of Florida. Nellie, unwilling to be separated from her beloved Willie again, accompanied her husband. While there she became nationally recognized for her extensive work in relief for soldiers. She single-handedly organized care for the National Guard soldiers who were exposed to malaria, typhoid fever, and dysentery at the camp.

When a group of ill soldiers was being transferred by train from Florida to Indiana, Nellie was quite concerned. She wondered who would provide care for these men on the long journey home. When there was no evident answer, Nellie decided she would go along with them herself, feeding them brandy and warm milk to sustain them as they made their way home.

On September 11, 1912, William Gordon died, and Nellie was said to never be the same. She mourned his passing more deeply with every new day. In fact, her family feared for her very sanity. Nellie's daughter, Juliette wrote a letter to her brother, Arthur. In the letter she mentioned their mother had always made one fact clear - she considered her main focus in life her marriage to William W. Gordon II. Although Nellie loved and cared for her children, her priority was always Willie.

> *"...she never pretended for a moment that he was not her first and last love, and we as nothing by comparison... Maternal love is the inheritance of the ages, but love such as Mamma gave him was a personal tribute." (from a letter Juliette wrote to her brother Arthur, c. 1912)*

After the death of her beloved husband, there seemed to be many indications that Nellie would never regain her former self.

A book found in the Gordon library on Spiritualism causes one to wonder whether Nellie believed in some tenants of that particular faith. Nellie appeared eager to join Willie in death, as she shared these ominous words in a letter to her cousin:

> "...here I remain, very much against my will, for there is nothing I so sincerely desire in this world as to get out of it."

Nellie was eighty-one years old when she penned this letter, and restless to meet her maker in the afterlife. She and Willie were inseparable in this life, and she wished for them to, once again, be together in the next.

In February of 1917, Nellie suffered a series of heart attacks. These episodes left her bedridden and gravely ill. She had good days and bad days. On one day, as she reflected on her mortality, she managed some final words to her daughter-in-law, Ellie, in which she said,

> "When I die, I don't want anybody to wear mourning. I don't want any tears. I shall be so happy to be with my Willie again, everybody should celebrate!"

Nellie's children were called to her bedside by the doctor to say their final goodbyes on February 22, 1917. Their mother was quickly slipping away and she would be gone by morning.

Nellie's son Arthur and his wife Margaret were gathered with the others at the bedside. Margaret quietly bid farewell to her mother-in-law and left to wait in the room that happened to be the former bedroom of the late General William Gordon.

She silently sat contemplating that imminent moment when Arthur would come to tell her that Nellie had passed away. Not more than a few minutes had gone by when, to Margaret's amazement, she looked up to see her deceased father-in-law come out of his wife's bedroom! He was, as Margaret recalled, dressed in the gray suit which had been his favorite to wear for business. She claimed William appeared serene and composed, with a happy expression on his lips. He passed through his old room and didn't seem to notice her. To her astonishment, he exited into the hallway. Dumbfounded, Margaret watched William's retreating back as he descended the front staircase.

A moment later, Arthur came to inform Margaret that his mother had just passed away. In utter shock, Margaret told her husband that she had just seen his father, General Gordon, only moments ago. Perplexed, Arthur felt Margaret must have been overcome by grief and stress. He told his wife it was obvious she must have fallen asleep and been dreaming.

While Margaret continued to insist it had really happened, they walked downstairs to meet the Gordon's butler. He was a former slave who had been with the family for as long as anyone could remember. With sadness in his voice, the elderly butler asked, "Is Ole Miss gone?" When they told him that, yes indeed, Mrs. Gordon had passed away, tears quickly filled his eyes. Then, to the surprise of both Margaret and Arthur, he went on to inform them that just before they came down, he saw General Gordon, wearing his favorite gray suit, descend the stairs and go out the front door. He appeared just as did in the days before his death, when the carriage would pick him up and take him to the Exchange. The butler remarked that he looked very well and very happy indeed! "I thought you'd like to know the General come fetch her hisself, suh," the old butler continued somberly.

Many years after Nellie's death, Juliette's niece, Daisy Gordon Lawrence, penned an account given by the children who had gathered at the bedside. They reported at the moment of their mother's death, she suddenly sat up in bed and held out her arms as if beckoning to an unseen visitor. In that moment, she appeared like a blushing new bride glimpsing her groom at the altar. Was Nellie seeing her beloved from beyond the veil? Nellie may have smiled as she took her last breath. She would finally be reunited in eternity with her darling Willie. This story seems to prove that Willie could not move on to the next life without the woman who meant the most to him. He had waited for his wife, Nellie, to join him.

Willie Gordon's spirit, along with the spirit of his beloved Nellie, continue to inhabit the family home. Nellie has been seen frequently by those who are employed at the Juliette Gordon Low birthplace; in the halls, on the veranda overlooking the courtyard, and strolling the garden pathways. People have seen her sitting at the kitchen table in a long blue floral dressing gown. Even though the piano is not in working order, they have heard Nellie, an accomplished musician, playing a haunting melody as she continues to visit her home.

Guides report hearing footsteps on the stairs and throughout the hallways as they lock up for the day. One guide had an unsettling encounter at the Gordon family home. Upon returning to the empty house to retrieve her personal belongings from an upstairs bedroom, she came face to face with Nellie Gordon. She recognized it was Mrs. Gordon from the portrait hanging in the library.

Workers report sometimes things seem to move of their own accord. Items reported missing by employees will magically reappear in an entirely different location a couple of days later. Perhaps these items aren't placed exactly as Nellie may have wished? Many of those employed at the Girl Scout National Center feel the ghosts of the Gordon family remain at the place they loved best.

The home is not the only place haunted by a member of the Gordon family. In 1886, Juliette Gordon married William Mackay Low, the son of prominent cotton plantation owner Andrew Low. William inherited his family's estate upon the death of his father. This became the home of Juliette and William Low. The Andrew Low house is located in downtown Savannah, just a few blocks from Juliette's childhood home and is open for tours. Juliette Gordon Low passed away in 1927 in the upstairs bedroom of her home. Passersby report seeing an old woman sitting on a rocking chair peering from an upstairs bedroom window. It is known that this was the chair in which Juliette spent much of her time towards the end of her life. She'd sit for hours watching people as they gathered on the square just outside her home.

What did Juliette Gordon Low see from her bedroom window? Madison Square, the scenic place that she spent so much time admiring, is considered one of the most haunted outdoor places in Savannah. Many battles from the Revolutionary War were waged on these very grounds. The square, surrounded today by beautiful stately homes, is a destination of historical meaning for those who visit the city.

During the building of these now historic homes surrounding Madison square, the bodies of buried British soldiers were disinterred from their final resting place. This land would have been the battlefield where they fell, casualties of the War for Independence waged by this original colony of the United States. Perhaps the tall, dark, shadowy figures seen lurking in the park are the residual energy of those soldiers whose eternal rest was disturbed. A walk through this square at night is sure to be unforgettable.

The Sorrel-Weed house, known as Shady Corner, is one such historic home that sits on Madison Square. There are numerous reports of paranormal activity at this property, including glowing handprints seen on the basement wall visible only in ultraviolet light. Items in the house are known to move as if touched by otherworldly hands. Photos of ghostly children have been captured. Voices have been heard when no one is speaking...at least no one of a human nature.

Savannah is considered by many to be America's most haunted city. Plan a visit to this historic metropolis to experience their many haunted places, and Savannah's most well-known ghostly love story. If you don't mind a little spooky activity, a stop at the home of William and Nellie Gordon should surely be considered for your next exploration of what might lie beyond the grave.

DEADLY LOVE

Evelyn Nesbit, The Gibson Girl

There are some criminal trials that are so salacious, so tantalizing, they captivate an entire nation (think O.J. Simpson or The Menendez Brothers). The story lives on in infamy, long after the judge bangs the final gavel.

In 1906, one such story made headlines across the nation. This is the true tale of deadly jealousy and lost innocence. It's a volatile mixture of money, power, love, and revenge. There is no happy ending for this colorful cast of characters, only the echoes of the ghosts left behind.

It was a tragic love triangle that led to cold-blooded murder. Millionaire architect Stanford White was shot dead by the husband of his former lover, a beautiful young girl named Evelyn Nesbit. Newspapers called it the "trial of the century." This case exposed the darker side of America's Gilded Age.

This incredible true-life story inspired two Hollywood films: 1955's "The Girl in the Red Velvet Swing," starring Farley Granger, Ray Milland, and Joan Collins as Evelyn Nesbit, and 1981's Oscar-nominated blockbuster, "Ragtime," featuring James Cagney and Elizabeth McGovern.

Fourteen-year-old Florence Evelyn Nesbit (known as Evelyn) moved with her family from Tarentum, Pennsylvania to New York City in 1901. The auburn-haired beauty had no trouble finding work as a model and muse. She had a bewitching allure that was always in demand.

Evelyn's image was everywhere - postcards, photographs, advertisements. She was the feminine ideal, the Gibson Girl. Evelyn was an instant star - America's first real supermodel. She wasn't just a pretty face; she could sing and dance as well. Evelyn landed a few chorus line roles on Broadway, including a part in the production of *Floradora*.

Evelyn was a rare combination of innocence and beauty that teetered on the edge of blossoming sexuality. The moral compass of the nation was transitioning from the restrictive Victorian Era to a more liberating one. Evelyn Nesbit embodied the eroticism and sensuality that had been stifled for decades.

The teenage glamour girl turned the heads of many suitors, most several years her senior. She caught the eye of forty-seven-year-old Stanford White, a married millionaire socialite. White's architectural designs helped shape the New York skyline. His buildings became the towering icons of Manhattan. One of his most famous projects was the original Madison Square Garden.

White rubbed shoulders with the Vanderbilts and Carnegies of New York High Society. He had luxurious apartment suites inside the Garden Tower and on W. 24th St., right above the FAO Schwarz Toy Store. In one apartment, White had a large adult size red velvet swing bolted to the ceiling. This was not a toy; it was a voyeuristic prop. The infamous swing would symbolize young Evelyn Nesbit's loss of innocence.

Deadly Love

White had a taste for excess; the best that money could buy. He surrounded himself with beautiful things, including beautiful women. He was a notorious womanizer. He was known to invite young girls to his apartment where he would wine, dine, and ultimately seduce them. Disturbing rumors circulated about White. Some claimed he engaged in illicit acts of sexual deviance with numerous young women. Were they victims or willing consorts? That depended on whose version you believe. Regardless of the truth, no one dared question White's behavior.

Stanford White pursued Evelyn relentlessly, but she refused his romantic advances, at first. She did, however, accept his financial help. White was, for all intents and purposes, her "sugar daddy." He showered her with expensive gifts and used his influence to boost her career. The affluent architect had the support of Evelyn's mother who encouraged the relationship for her own benefit. Evelyn's earnings were the main source of income for the Nesbit family. She had an enormous financial responsibility. A wealthy man like Stanford White substantially lessened the burden on his teenage protégée.

After about a year, White's tenacity paid off. He invited Evelyn, now sixteen, to dinner one evening while her mother was out of town. After dinner, White entertained the young girl in the "mirror room," a small bedchamber covered floor to ceiling with mirrors. Evelyn drank a copious amount of champagne and eventually passed out. When she awoke, Stanford White was lying naked next to her in bed. Intoxicated, she had succumbed to White, losing her virginity and her dignity. White swore her to secrecy. Evelyn, embarrassed and ashamed, had no intention of telling anyone.

Some suggest Evelyn was younger than sixteen at the time of her encounter with White. Her mother may have lied about her daughter's age to get around New York child labor laws. That would make Evelyn closer to fourteen when she first met White.

Evelyn Nesbit became Stanford White's pet project and his mistress. During this time, she endured the continual affections of the much older man. He wielded a mysterious power she could neither deny nor escape. Sinister rumors circulated in hushed conversations about their May-December romance. They said White forced Evelyn to sit naked on the infamous red velvet swing. She swayed to and fro in an erotic dance, all for the perverse pleasure of a man who was, to many, a monster.

One can only speculate why Evelyn stayed with White for as long as she did. Maybe she valued a life of privilege and creature comforts more than her dignity. Or maybe the young girl felt powerless in the hands of her older, wiser benefactor. Her mother may have forced her to stay with the millionaire to ensure the financial survival of the family.

Or it could be that Evelyn actually fell in love with White. He was, after all, the driving force in her personal and professional life. She had other options but chose to remain as White's companion and concubine. Evelyn was entangled in an extremely dysfunctional and codependent relationship.

But nothing lasts forever. Eventually, Stanford White moved on to other young girls, other conquests. Evelyn was free from his imperious grasp. Instead of relief, Evelyn felt used, like she was being pushed aside for a younger version of herself. To his credit, White didn't abandon her completely. He managed to stay as a strong influence in her life, even providing some financial support. They often ran in the same social circles.

Although no longer lovers, White was apprehensive of any suitor who got too close to Evelyn. He was always protective and kept a watchful eye on her.

The fairytale took another turn when Evelyn met Harry Kendall Thaw. He was a handsome man in his thirties, filled with confidence and arrogance. The son of a wealthy railroad tycoon, he was a spoiled playboy who did little in the way of work. He was bold, boisterous, and larger than life.

But Harry K. Thaw had a dark side too...

Thaw was a sexual sadist with an obsessive personality. His wealth kept him out of trouble with the law, but he had a sullied reputation with the ladies. Some women he dated claimed he beat, belittled, and tortured them. He had a preference for young chorus girls. Thaw became infatuated with Evelyn after seeing her perform in a show. He was used to getting what he wanted, and he wanted Evelyn. He wooed the naive beauty with the same relentless determination as Stanford White.

And there was something else...

Harry Thaw despised Stanford White. Beyond simple hatred, he was consumed with animosity toward the older man. Not only was White a romantic rival, but a social obstacle as well. Thaw believed that White black balled him, kept him out of certain social clubs and events. Thaw felt snubbed by the self-made industry giant and his wealthy powerful friends. The millionaire heir's money couldn't buy him access to the exclusive circles he was so desperate to be a part of.

Thaw had other issues as well. He had an explosive temper and a debilitating drug problem. The mentally unstable man was also a jealous one. When Stanford White discovered Thaw had his eye on Evelyn, he warned her to stave off his pursuits. White knew that Thaw was trouble, but could never have foreseen how dangerous he truly was.

Harry K. Thaw coveted Evelyn Nesbit as much as he wanted to ruin Stanford White. He stalked her like a hungry predator in a custom-tailored suit. He came to see her perform in one show more than three dozen times. His pursuit of Evelyn went on for two years. Wherever she went, Thaw was there. His amorous intentions were perfectly clear.

Thaw proposed to her on several occasions. Evelyn turned him down each time. She may have been more inclined to accept his offer but for one insurmountable obstacle. He had a strong notion of marital purity, at least on the part of the wife. Evelyn knew that Thaw expected her to be a virgin before marriage. Stanford White had made that impossible. Thaw continued his pursuit undaunted.

Evelyn fell sick in 1903. She was frail and weak while recovering from some sort of operation. Some believed it was an illegal abortion, but it may have been a simple appendectomy. Thaw invited her and her mother, Mrs. Nesbit, on a whirlwind "recuperative" European vacation that was anything but restful. The trip was an exhausting journey led by an increasingly unstable Thaw. While abroad, he hoped to charm Evelyn once and for all. He repeatedly asked for her hand in marriage but still she said no. Her constant refusals were driving his rage and madness. He was desperate to find out why Evelyn wouldn't accept his proposal.

During the trip, Evelyn's mother became ill and traveled to London to recover. This was Thaw's golden opportunity. With Mrs. Nesbit out of the way, he could be more aggressive with his quarry. Once he had Evelyn alone, Thaw continued his barrage of proposals. When she refused, he insisted on knowing why. This time he wouldn't settle until he got the truth. His proposal wasn't a romantic gesture or declaration of love. It was more like an ultimatum given by a schoolyard bully.

Unfettered, Thaw somehow managed to coerce an admission out of her.

Evelyn reluctantly confessed she had a physical relationship with Stanford White. She told him about unchaperoned visits to the Garden Suite and the night in the "mirror room." The news crushed Thaw. Evelyn Nesbit was damaged goods, but he still believed he loved her.

Harry K. Thaw's mother, Mary Copley Thaw, didn't approve of her son's choice in women. She heard rumors the couple planned to wed while in Europe. She was furious. She vowed to cut him off from the family fortune and decrease his allowance if he married a chorus girl. Mary Thaw tried in vain to save her son from such an unsavory choice. But threats did little to deter him. In the end, her devotion to her son outweighed the embarrassment of having a showgirl for a daughter-in-law.

Evelyn Nesbit, concerned for her future and her financial security, finally relented. She accepted Harry K. Thaw's proposal of marriage. Spirit broken and confidence wavering, she believed Thaw was her best option.

Evelyn Nesbit and Harry Thaw married on April 4, 1905. The couple retreated to Elmhurst, the family's 7,000 square foot country manor located in Loretto, Pennsylvania. The magnificent three-story home was the gem of Cambria County, about 80 miles east of Pittsburgh. The English Tudor mansion sat on 130 acres of land offering pristine views of the Allegheny Mountains. The couple lived under the ever-critical eye of her new husband's mother. The matriarch of the Thaw fortune thought little of her son's bride. Evelyn spent her time at Elmhurst trying to adjust to her mother-in-law's idea of who she should be. The mansion felt like a dungeon, not a dream home.

From poverty to privilege, America's Sweetheart, the Gibson Girl, was more a prisoner than a princess. There wasn't much of a honeymoon period for the couple. Evelyn somberly endured her husband's unpredictable mood swings and violent outbursts. He tortured her, demeaned her, and kept her away from the things she loved.

Harry Thaw drifted deeper and deeper into a dark, downward spiral. He had an obsessive need to avenge his wife's honor. Stanford White defiled his Evelyn. Madness, addiction, and with a sick sense of husbandly duty, Thaw was determined to destroy his nemesis. His opportunity came when the couple visited New York City later that summer.

On June 25, 1906, Harry Kendall Thaw and his wife attended a rooftop musical at Madison Square Garden. The event was filled with New York's elite, theater lovers, and those just out for an enjoyable evening of entertainment. Stanford White was among the theater guests that night. Thaw was visibly agitated throughout the performance.

Evelyn noticed White sitting at a table close to the stage. She was concerned about a possible confrontation between her husband and her former lover. After the show, Evelyn tried to coerce Thaw out of the theater. Instead, he made a beeline toward his nemesis.

Thaw walked brazenly up to White and shot him three times twice in the head and once in the shoulder. "He ruined my wife!" exclaimed Thaw as he pulled the trigger on his revolver.

Stanford White was dead on the roof of Madison Square Garden, the same building which made him a giant of New York. Onlookers were shocked by the shameless actions of the gunwielding madman.

Thaw was arrested for murder. He spent six months in jail before the trial began in January of 1907. Thaw's defense was that Stanford White deserved to die. He was nothing more than a sadistic child molester and sexual predator.

Evelyn testified at the trial that Stanford White raped her and was every bit the monster that Thaw made him out to be. She was victimized by White and her loving husband was only defending her honor. She expertly played the role of a loving, devoted wife. Mary Thaw most likely paid off Evelyn for her testimony.

The trial made headlines all over the country. The proceedings were a travesty of justice - more theater than litigation. It was a series of character attacks on White, filled with eye-witness accounts of his sadistic habits. This was a crime of passion, a man defending the honor of his love. The victim was being prosecuted, not the man who murdered him. Due to the widespread publicity, the judge ordered the jury sequestered during the proceedings. This was the first time on record that a jury had ever been completely kept from the public.

The trial resulted in a hung jury. Thaw was returned to prison and retried the following January. The second trial found him not guilty by reason of insanity. Harry Thaw was sent to the Matteawan State Hospital for the Criminally Insane.

Thaw escaped the hospital in 1913 and fled to Canada. He was captured and sent back in 1914. With the help of his money and connections, he was eventually declared sane and released in July 1915.

Thaw filed for divorce from Evelyn as soon as he was freed. Was this because he no longer loved her, or because he no longer needed her? Had he ever loved her or was she merely a pawn in his plan to destroy Stanford White?

Evelyn was now finally free as well.

Harry K. Thaw continued on a self-destructive road of madness and violence. He enticed a nineteen-year-old California boy named Fred Gump to visit him in

New York. He lured the boy with the promise of a free education.

Not long after he arrived, Thaw attacked the boy with a whip. He held him prisoner in his hotel, treating him like a dog. He had the Gump on a leash and made him walk around on all fours. Thaw made the boy sleep on the floor and call him "master." Gump managed to escape and reported his encounter to authorities. Harry Thaw unsuccessfully attempted suicide. Money couldn't buy him out of this mess. He was arrested and sent to another insane asylum where he remained until 1924. Thaw eventually passed away in 1947.

As for Evelyn Nesbit, she never found the happiness she so desperately desired. Tragedy followed her for the rest of her life. She kept working, sometimes on Vaudeville as an entertainer. She married again but soon that relationship also ended in divorce. As fate would have it, Evelyn later became an addict herself and suffered from recurring bouts of depression.

In 1955, Hollywood capitalized on her misery and bought the rights to her life story. This was the basis for the film, "The Girl in the Red Velvet Swing." Although only loosely based on the facts, the film tells the tragic tale of America's beloved Gibson Girl.

Evelyn Nesbit died on January 17, 1967. In her memoirs, she claimed Stanford White was the only man who ever had her heart. He wasn't the monster people made him out to be. To quote the movie that fictionalized her story, "She loved a man she could not marry and married a man she could not love."

Evelyn Nesbit is the embodiment of tragic beauty. She is forever immortalized on film, in books, and throughout history. It's no wonder she lives on as a somber spirit, decades after her death.

Evelyn's ghost haunts Elmhurst, the Pennsylvania estate she shared with her murderous husband, Harry

Thaw. Her short time at Elmhurst was not a happy one, but it was still home. She has returned to seek refuge and absolution.

The Elmhurst estate changed hands several times over the decades. It was once a church retreat as well as a restaurant and concert hall. Al and Linda Lewis purchased the property in 1989 to be used as a private residence. They quickly realized they were not alone.

The paranormal activity is evident to both visitors and staff. Caretakers who stayed in a trailer on the property reported many strange occurrences. They've heard phantom footsteps, mysterious banging, and the eerie disembodied voice of a man calling out. The thermostat would inexplicably go up and down. They've witnessed a misty form that looks like a woman in a wide-brimmed hat.

The activity continues in the main house as well. A luminous female apparition, believed to be Evelyn, has been spotted on many occasions. Her lonely spirit glides down the corridors of the mansion. Her sullen image often materializes in mirrors or peers out of upstairs windows. The sorrowful sound of a woman crying comes from empty rooms. Doors open and close by themselves. Unexplainable electrical anomalies plague the old mansion. They say Evelyn's ghost wanders the beautiful gardens and grounds of Elmhurst.

A more physical spirit dwells in the house at times. It has been known to open the front door after it has been locked. Some invisible force manipulates the kitchen stove, turning it on at times. Once, a little girl was inexplicably pulled out of a chair by her hair.

There is a road not far from the mansion where an unusual phenomenon transpires. Travelers often see a beautiful woman in a long dress walking along the asphalt. Her clothes seem characteristic of a past era. She appears melancholy and dazed, moving slowly across the pavement. Some stop and ask the woman if she needs help, or if they can offer her a ride. She turns and reveals an ashen face with dark, empty eyes. She gets into the car and says, "Take me home." When asked where she lives, she answers, "Elmhurst." As soon as the car starts to drive off, the mysterious woman disappears, vanishing into thin air.

She is always described the same way; a beautiful auburnhaired woman in a long white dress who looks lost and heartbroken. The light hits her face in a most unusual way, making her seem ethereal and out of focus. She evokes a gentle sadness as she asks softly speaks.

The phantom hitchhiker that haunts the highway and the halls of Elmhurst is Evelyn Nesbit. She is eternally alone, searching for love and the innocence stolen from her in life.

FORBIDDEN LOVE

Sabina And Orwin

*T*he following love story is widely accepted as fact by
the people of Oldcastle and those who are familiar
with Ross Castle. Although The Black Baron (Richard
Nugent) can be traced through deeds and documents,
information on his descendants is sketchy. Little could
be found historically to verify the existence of Sabina and
Orwin, although there are numerous accounts of their
ghosts haunting the property. Whether they be real or
fictional characters, there is no denying the paranormal
activity attributed to their lovelorn spirits.

Ireland is a place of undeniable beauty. Its palate is
an array of vibrant green fields and azure blue waters.
The aptly named Emerald Isle is the jewel of the United
Kingdom. It sits as a testament to nature's magnificence
and diversity. Surrounded by a cold, heartless sea,
Ireland's unique geography makes it a paradise or
purgatory, depending on the season and weather
conditions. The tempestuous ocean attacks the rocky
cliffs with an angry determination. A subtle yet powerful
vibration radiates from very soul of this awe-inspiring
land.

Today, Ireland is an enchanting haven for families with deep generational roots, or a picturesque vacation spot for thousands of camera- ready tourists. It is a place of pride and of peace. But it wasn't always like that. The history of Ireland is written in blood. Thousands of years of violence and death have stained the landscape deep into its core. The sins of the past are covered by a blanket of soft green grass.

Evidence of human habitation in Ireland dates back to before the Mesolithic era. Thousands of years before the Roman empire swept across Europe, native tribes made the unforgiving terrain a viable homestead. The Celts were a people that flourished during the Iron Age, a time lasting approximately from 500 BCE to 500 CE. They practiced polytheism, a belief in many gods. It was during this period that the druids established themselves as the predominate religious congregation. By the 6th century, their Celtic pagan beliefs had morphed into what we would see as pre-Christian values.

Though isolated, Ireland was not beyond the reach of foreign invaders. The island was vulnerable to the ruthless, conquering tribes of the Vikings. The vastness of the open ocean was mastered by the stalwart explorers who made their way from Scandinavia to the northern coast of Ireland around 795 CE. Their ability to cross great distances and precisely navigate the sea in self- powered and elaborately carved ships was a testament to Viking determination and strength. Brutal and unyielding, they had a profound and often severe influence on the Irish culture that lasted for hundreds of years.

From the time of the Norman invasion in the latter part of the 12th century, Ireland was ruled by England. Norman lords fought with the ruling English king, keeping Ireland in a constant state of upheaval. Celtic

Irish clans struggled to maintain control of the northern and western regions of Ireland, while the English held areas that extended east. Their interest in Ireland was focused mainly on four counties referred to as the Colony, ending at an area known as the Pale. The Pale was a swath of land west of Dublin that ended at Lough Sheelin. For clarification, "lough" is the Gaelic word for lake. The border of Lough Sheelin was always a tense and tightly held plot of land often challenged by opposing parties. The Nugent family, loyal to the English rule, controlled the Pale for centuries.

The English involvement led to a volatile political climate with the people of Ireland, who very much resented the foreigners and their superior beliefs. In 1541, Henry VIII proclaimed himself "King of Ireland" and tried to force the reformation on its people. He set the stage for years of upheaval and conflict. Civil unrest and political turmoil were the daily norm for the people of Ireland. Some of these battles became legendary in the annals of Irish lore. Between the epic tales of brave warriors and bloody outcomes, we find glimmers of light and hope. Between the hate and rage of war, we find true tales of devotion and romance.

In the midst of the madness, love prevails.

The castles of 16th century Ireland were not places of grandeur and opulence. Those who ruled needed strong fortifications to fend off their enemies. And there was no shortage of enemies. An ancient village sat to the south of the River Inny as it entered Lough Sheelin. In the small community of Ross, located in County Meath (an area north of present day Dublin) lived a man named Richard Nugent, 12th Lord of Delvin. In 1532, Nugent, known to the people of Ross as "The Black Baron," built a suitable stronghold called the Castle of Ross. It wasn't a massive Medieval monstrosity but it was secure and imposing, well-suited for a man of his stature. The

Castle of Ross sat nestled on the southern shores of Lough Sheelin.

The Black Baron was said to be a man with a hardened heart, thus earning his formidable nickname. He was loyal to the English crown, for the king had granted him titleship to the land. The local Irish clans resented losing their ancestral home to the King's appointed lords. Keeping the peace was always a delicate and often bloody matter. As a ruler, the Black Baron was a force to be reckoned with. He was ruthless, quick to anger, and eager to reign down what he believed to be swift justice. Those around him knew it was better to stay out of his way when he was in a foul mood. Stories of his brutality were legendary to the people of County Meath.

One famous tale illustrates the Baron's dark personality. Whether it be a factual account or an exaggerated anecdote, the people of Ross believed it to be a cautionary tale not to be taken lightly. One day a woman who lived in the village was busy working in her kitchen, making bread for her family. She placed a freshly baked loaf on her window sill to let it cool a bit. The inviting aroma attracted a hungry dog who happened to be nearby. The opportunistic dog quickly snatched the bread from the window and slipped away, unseen by anyone in the house. Moments later, the woman saw her bread was gone and realized it had been stolen. She shouted, "Thief! Thief!" raising the alarm of her neighbors.

They immediately set out to find the culprit, assuming it was a man, not a dog. The Black Baron was on a hunting expedition with a group of his men at the time. Word of the stolen bread spread quickly until it eventually reached the Baron's ear. He was appalled at the emboldened act. He would not stand for such a crime in his land! The angry entourage switched from hunting game to hunting a thief. Soon they came across a stranger, a traveler, peacefully napping under a tree. The man was a poor beggar; someone who would be a likely suspect for the stolen food. The Baron abruptly woke the man and questioned him, accusing him of theft. The bewildered man had no idea what was happening and professed his innocence to any wrongdoing. The denial only enraged the Black Baron. He instructed his men to build a makeshift gallows. The stranger was hung on the spot.

The Black Baron believed he had the right to demand whatever punishment he deemed proper. His actions sent a message to any would-be lawbreakers that he was not one to be toyed with or lied to, even over something as trivial as a loaf of bread. Justice was at the will and whim of the lord of the land and no one dare question his authority.

But the haste of both the town and the Baron led to a tragic miscarriage of justice. The partially eaten bread was discovered a while later. The teeth marks on the loaf pointed to a shocking realization - the man they hung was not the culprit. It was evident that the real thief was an animal, most likely the hungry stray dog that had been spotted in the area.

The people of Ross were ashamed of their actions and for the resulting death of the stranger. The repentant villagers couldn't bare to look at the place of execution. They planted a tree where the gallows stood, in memory of the innocent man who lost his life to the anger of the Black Baron. Did the Baron feel any remorse for the horrific mistake? No one knows for sure. But the tree still stands today, reminding future generations of the perils of prejudice.

According to widely accepted Irish lore, the Black Baron raised a family at the Castle of Ross. He may have been tough and callous on the outside, but he had one soft spot; his beautiful daughter, Sabina. She was the light of his life. She brought out the goodness buried deep inside his hardened soul. The Baron adored his daughter and took great measures to keep her safe. She was as delicate as she was beautiful, falling ill on many occasions. Sabina's frail constitution was worrisome for her family and those charged with her care.

It wasn't just her sickly nature that concerned Sabina's father. He feared her life could be in danger just by being the daughter of Richard Nugent, 12th Lord of Delvin. There was no shortage of warring clans that would love to get their hands on such a valuable part of the Baron's estate. Knowing that Sabina was a target for his enemies, the Baron made sure she was under constant supervision.

Sabina enjoyed long leisurely walks along the shores of Lough Sheelin, chaperoned of course, by someone of her father's choosing. She cherished these times and always greeted the townsfolk with her bright smile and gentle spirit. The people of Ross adored Sabina, despite her familial connection to a brutal English lord. As fearful as they were of the Black Baron, they felt genuine love for such a kind and lovely girl.

Over the years, Sabina's happiness turned to loneliness. As she blossomed from a carefree child to a young woman, she longed for the same things all teenage girls desire. The constant company of her governess or maid servant was not the companionship she yearned for. Her thoughts turned to young men, although the Baron kept most well out of eyesight. She knew if she was ever to find love, or even just a bit of romance, she would need to ditch the babysitter.

Sabina was smart, resourceful, and determined to break away from the confines of the castle. She cleverly found ways to sneak out undetected, thus enjoying a bit of freedom and adventure. The potential danger of her actions only made these outings more exciting for the wily teenager. Sabina was blissfully unconcerned about consequences or the thought of angering her father.

It was on one of these outings that Sabina met a handsome young man named Orwin. She felt the flutter that young girls do when in the presence of someone they find attractive. An immediate wave of emotion washed over them as they talked. Orwin was captivated by Sabina's effervescent personality and precocious demeanor. After spending considerable time together, Sabina had to head home. Sabina and Orwin vowed to meet at the same spot again - a promise they kept unbeknownst to their families. Their blossoming romance erupted into an all-consuming affair of the heart. It wasn't long before the young couple realized they were deeply in love.

Their relationship was problematic for many reasons. Sabina was forbidden to be away from the castle without a chaperone, so her secret excursions would come to light. And meeting with a boy unsupervised? Scandalous! Also, Sabina was the daughter of an English lord. She was expected to marry someone of English blood and at least of equal social and economic stature. Orwin was Irish. He was also the son of a rival chieftain, an O'Reilly, someone whom the Baron considered an enemy. Their love story was doomed from the start.

The two lovebirds were determined to be together, no matter the cost. They knew their families would never approve of their union, and no amount of pleading would sway opinions to their favor. There was only one thing for Sabina and Orwin to do. They must run away together, far from the clutches of their heartless fathers. It was their best and possibly only chance at happiness.

After little planning and a lot of unrealistic dreams, Sabina and Orwin decided to elope. They embarked on a most dangerous plan. Under cover of night, Sabina snuck away from the Castle of Ross and headed to the cold dark shores of Lough Sheelin. Orwin was there, waiting anxiously for his love. They boarded a small row boat. Their plan was to cross the lough and escape unnoticed by the locals. They needed to get as far away from the Black Baron's territory as possible. Together, they rowed madly, trying to get across the water before the sunrise.

Only moments into their escape, a great storm arose over the lough. Thunderous waves rocked the boat as heavy rain poured down on the frightened couple. The storm was like a manifestation of the Black Baron's anger - violent and unrelenting. The small boat was tossed around like a child's toy as the winds screamed menacingly in their ears. They were no match for Mother Nature and Ireland's unpredictable weather. The tiny boat overturned and broke apart, throwing Sabina and Orwin into the frigid water.

The Baron was alerted that Sabina was missing. His concern grew to horror when he learned a severe storm had fallen upon the lough. He sent his men out to find his little girl and bring her home safely. Luckily, Sabina was spotted just as her boat broke apart. She struggled helplessly in the water before finally sinking beneath the waves. The Baron's men reached her just in time. She was rescued, pulled from the water before she drowned. She was taken to the castle were nurses attended to her injuries. Sabina lay in a coma for three days before waking. Orwin was not so lucky. No sign of the young man could be found. He had been swallowed by the ravenous storm. After the winds and rain subsided, the lough fell silent once again. Shortly thereafter, Orwin's lifeless body washed up on shore.

When Sabina finally awoke, her immediate concern was for Orwin. If she survived, then surely he must have as well. She had to retain even just a morsel of hope that he was alive! When she learned the news that her love was dead, she nearly collapsed. She felt as if the air had been sucked out of her as the blood drained from her face. Sabina fell into a deep depression. Her heart was shattered and her soul empty. Her love was gone and any chance for happiness lost. She was destined to be forever under the heavy thumb of her father, who would surely never let her out of his sight again. Sabina was absolutely devastated. She lost the will to live and refused to eat or drink, no matter how much her father pleaded. She withered away slowly and painfully before eventually dying of a broken heart.

The Black Baron lost the one person that he loved more than anything. Sabina was his joy, his greatest achievement, his legacy. It is said that in his life he only had two regrets; hanging an innocent man, and losing his daughter. People can only speculate what was in his heart and if he truly felt any remorse for his deeds. But the ghost stories surrounding the Black Baron seem to corroborate this theory.

Nugent descendants continued to occupy the Castle of Ross for generations. Additions and renovations were made to keep the historic property properly maintained. Today the property is called Ross Castle. It is conveniently located about an hour from Dublin proper - far enough but not too far from the bustling metropolitan capital of Ireland. Now a beautiful B & B, Ross Castle welcomes guests from all over the world. The property has six bedrooms, five and a half baths, and includes a 500 year old Norman Keep. Ross Castle attracts globetrotting tourists as well as Irish locals. It's been modernized, yet still holds its authentic historic charm.

Some come for the scenery, but many come for the ghosts. Ross Castle is said to be haunted by several spirits - namely the Black Baron, his daughter Sabina, and her ill-fated lover Orwin. People may speculate if the story of the doomed lovers is true, but few can deny the ghostly activity attributed to the couple.

Some of the most telling encounters happen inside Ross Castle. The current owners welcome travelers to their beautiful piece of Irish history. They embrace the paranormal and invite people to come and experience the castle for themselves. Ghost hunters and those curious about haunted history put Ross Castle at the top of their list of favorite places.

Visitors claim they've had remarkable paranormal encounters all throughout the beautifully restored castle. From phantom footsteps to strange orbs of light, there is no shortage of unexplainable phenomenon. Poltergeist activity is common, ranging from drawers opening and closing to heavy doors slamming shut. A few people have claimed physical encounters with the ghosts that range from light touches to deliberate scratches. The sensation of being watched has chased more than one visiting guest running into the night. Psychic mediums sense a malevolent male spirit as well as a harmless, yet irritated female spirit that habitually make their presence known.

The majority of visual reports involve glimpses of a young girl, thin and pale, roaming inside the castle keep. She appears ethereal, cloaked in a translucent veil of light. She darts from room to room, as if in search of something...or someone. The apparition manifests in several areas of the castle, including the guest rooms, startling unsuspecting visitors. Her sorrowful cries echo through the thick stone corridors. They believe this is Sabina, desperate and heartbroken, mourning the loss of her love. Agonizing screams wake sleeping patrons from their beds in the middle of the night. Fearing someone in the castle is in danger, they hurriedly follow the alarming sounds. When they investigate, no source can be found. This activity is attributed to Sabina as well. It's as if she is reliving the moment she heard the news of Orwin's death.

Other spirits haunting the castle include Richard Nugent, 12th Lord of Delvin, aka the Black Baron. Some believe the Black Baron suffered the death of Sabina as payback for his evil deeds. He is now cursed to haunt the castle for eternity. His tortured ghost wanders the building at night, frantically searching for his beloved daughter. He radiates a powerful, ominous energy. A menacing shadow figure thought to be the Baron is seen lurking in the main areas of the castle. Run-ins with the dark entity keep paranormal enthusiasts on their toes.

The property around Lough Sheelin and the village of Oldcastle (the current name of the area) seem to be teeming with supernatural occurrences. The locals claim the shores of Lough Sheelin are extremely haunted. The area near the hanging tree is a hot-spot for paranormal activity. The tree may have been planted to honor the innocent man, but his spirit is not at rest. The apparition of a man is often spotted by the tree. Sometimes it looks as if he is peacefully sleeping under the shade, but other times he appears to be hanging from the thick branches above.

But the blue waters of Lough Sheelin are the most active. It is on these shores that the ghosts of doomed lovers spend their eternity. A small boat has been spotted on the lough during severe storms. Those who see it think the people on board are in distress and look on helplessly from the edge of the turbulent waters. The waves look as if they will surely capsize the small vessel. But just as suddenly as the storm appears, it is gone! Stillness takes its place. And the boat disappears as well, dissolving completely into the mist. No sign of the boat or its passengers is ever found. Are the spirits of Sabina and Orwin reliving the moment that ended their lives?

The heartbreaking tale of an English girl and an Irish boy resonate throughout the property of Ross Castle and beyond. Maybe their spirits splintered into many moments, some happy, some sad. Their story had a tragic ending, but their love survived the ages. Their ghosts continue to meet in secret, like they did so many times before. These were the happiest times, the precious few minutes when they dreamed of a future as husband and wife. One can hope that these are the most common paranormal encounters of Sabina and Orwin.

If you ever have the privilege to visit Ross Castle, beware of the spirit of the Black Baron. His ghost remains vigilant, keeping a close watch on his magnificent home and protecting it from outsiders. Or maybe he seeks redemption and forgiveness from his beloved daughter, and won't rest until she is at peace. When in County Meath, be sure to visit the shores of Lough Sheelin. Gaze upon the beauty and tranquility of this Irish treasure. When twilight comes, look closely at the water's edge. You may just catch a glimpse of two lovelorn spirits, walking hand-in-hand, laughing and smiling. Sabina Nugent and Orwin O'Reilly finally have in death the only thing they ever wanted in life - a chance to be together forever.

UNREQUITED LOVE
The Tragic Tale Of Louiza Fox

Louiza Fox, fair of face,
Full of wonder, full of grace.
Thomas Carr, filled with woe,
A cunning cad with a heart of snow.

- Written by Cathi Weber

Louiza Catharine Fox was just a young girl, considered by those around the town of Egypt, Ohio, to be beautiful and graceful. Soon to be fourteen years old, she was not considered a child but was not yet a woman. The future stretched out before her like an untraveled road – that is, until one fateful day when a man named Thomas David Carr came into her life.

The area of Egypt Valley, Ohio in Belmont County, was a vast agricultural mecca in 1869. This rural community consisted largely of farmers and coal miners. Coal was an important industry, and strip-mining was an easy way to claim the coal readily found in that region. Kirkwood Township, located in Egypt Valley, was home to Louiza Fox.

Louiza's parents, John and Mary Fox, along with her younger brother, William (Willie) were simple farmers. Louiza's older sister had already married and lived a short distance away with her husband. Her grandparents also lived close by in the next homestead over. She liked to visit them whenever she could. Louiza dreamed of the day she would marry and begin her life as someone's wife. Only time would reveal who her one true love would be.

Louiza was employed by the Robert Wallace family who lived in a town to the west of Kirkwood, called Sewellsville. In the nineteenth century, it was a common practice to "borrow" children from neighboring households if you didn't have any female offspring. These young girls, called domestic servants, would help with all the chores necessary to take care of the home.

Louiza was just thirteen when she went to work for the Wallaces. The hours of a servant-maid were long, bordering on fifteen hours a day. The Wallaces offered to have Louiza stay with them. The Foxes agreed, feeling this would be a safer alternative to making the daily two-mile trek from the Wallaces back to their family farm.

At the same time, Thomas Carr, a twenty-three-year-old Civil War veteran, formerly of West Virginia, was employed as a coal miner in Sewellsville. It so happened Bob Wallace was the brother-in-law of Thomas Carr. Thomas was a frequent visitor to the Wallace house. His visits increased significantly after meeting Louiza. He and the young, pretty maid struck up an easy friendship. Thomas was soon smitten with the sweet girl. He asked if she would consider keeping company with him, to which she complied with some degree of reluctance.

A brief amount of time passed before Thomas began his formal courtship of Louiza. Though she was flattered by the affections of the older man, she did not encourage him, and continued to keep their relationship one of friendship. Whenever Louiza would make a trip to visit her family at home, Thomas would accompany her. The Foxes were concerned with the attention the man was giving their daughter, and with the vast difference in their ages. Nonetheless, they saw no real reason the two could not remain friends. Thomas appeared to be genuinely concerned for Louiza's safety and felt she shouldn't walk home alone.

Soon, Louiza went to work for the Hunter family, the same people who employed Thomas. While she stayed there in domestic service, he came by daily on business. Their relationship continued as Thomas put further pressure on Louiza to marry him. He pledged his eternal love for Louiza. He stated if she could not be with him, perhaps they would both be better off dead. Mrs. Hunter, suspecting the girl was being coerced into strengthening her bond with Thomas, strongly urged Louiza against consorting with the man.

Louiza made sure her family knew that Thomas intended to marry her. She begged them to refuse their consent if he asked for her hand. Thomas, it seems, was not so easily deterred. He was determined she would be his wife. As soon as the opportunity presented itself, he met with Louiza's father to officially ask for permission to take her as his wife.

John Fox spent time in counsel with both his daughter and his family members. He weighed this proposal carefully, remembering Louiza had made it clear she did not wish to marry Thomas. Her mother chimed in to remind everyone of Louiza's young age. After some inquiries around town, her father found that Thomas was known for his infamous character and his propensity to react in fits of anger. He had been involved in several known assaults. His dealings with unsavory individuals were contemptible. Also, Thomas liked alcohol just a little too much.

John Fox firmly told Thomas the family would not allow this marriage. Louiza was but a child and not ready to even consider his proposal. The family also found him lacking in prospects.

Mrs. Fox tried to soften the blow by telling him that after he had been gainfully employed for some time, he could purchase some property and prove himself to be a worthy young man. It would make a difference if he were able to provide for their daughter. By then, a few years will have passed, and Louiza would be more mature. At which time, if Louiza was willing, marriage might be a possibility.

Thomas left the Fox home seeming to accept their decision. However, over the next few days he returned to his previous mindset. It was obvious that he had no intention of complying with the family's wishes. He renewed his declaration of love for the young girl. Thomas bestowed gifts upon Louiza, which made her feel uncomfortable. Not wanting to encourage him, she returned the gifts. This rejection of her suitor sealed her fate.

When her parents learned his passionate attentions towards their daughter had been renewed, they became concerned. Louiza's father sent her six-year-old brother, Willie, to fetch his sister from the Hunters. They wanted her close by for safety.

On January 21, 1869, the siblings started for home. A short while later they were surprised by the sudden appearance of Thomas. The jilted suitor was waiting for them, concealed by some brush at the side of the road. Thomas and Louiza continued to walk along, talking in subdued tones, until they reached the property of her grandparents. There, Louiza made up an excuse as to why they had to stop to visit her grandfather. She and

Willie rushed off to their grandparents' house, leaving Thomas standing by the road. They stayed for a while until she felt it safe to leave and continue the short walk home.

As they started down the path towards home, her brother curiously asked her why they had stopped to see their grandfather. She told him Thomas had threatened to harm her if she didn't marry him. Suddenly, they glimpsed Thomas just ahead, hiding behind a fence. He hurried over and fell into step with them once again. Whispered words of urgency floated over to little Willie's ears where he lagged just a few steps behind. He couldn't hear exactly what was being said, but felt they were in imminent danger.

When they were only a short distance from their farm, Thomas brutally grabbed Louiza and pushed her into a ditch near the road. He picked her up and threw her small body into the bank as she begged for her life. Willie cried for help as he ran as fast as he could towards home; his sister's ongoing screams echoed in his ears. The last thing Willie recalled seeing was Thomas reaching into his pocket and pulling out a straight razor.

Willie bolted up the road yelling out for his father. Together they ran as fast as they could back to the ditch where Louiza was last seen. They were too late. A scene of unimaginable horror unfolded before them. Her throat had been cut so deeply that her head was nearly severed from her body. Her breast and stomach were sliced open. Deep gashes across her hands and arms gave the appearance she had almost been dismembered. Louiza's life's blood ran out of her body, mingling like ruby tears with the water of the culvert. With horrified grief, John Fox glimpsed Thomas Carr running across the field, disappearing into the dusk.

The neighbors poured out of their homes upon hearing the commotion. They removed the girl's lifeless body from the gutter and took her home where she was laid on the kitchen table. The doctors assembled to prepare Louiza's remains for burial. Friends and family arrived to offer comfort and make a plan to apprehend the murderer. Darkness descended swiftly and the organized manhunt for the killer was postponed until the light of dawn.

In the meantime, Thomas wandered aimlessly through the black night of the countryside. He hiked about two miles making his way past area farms. At several, he inquired if they had a gun he could use for rabbit hunting. After many failed attempts, he finally arrived at the home of Mrs. Young, who gave him a rifle with one load. He urged her for more ammunition and she gave him one more shot. He thanked her and left with the firearm. He fully intended to return to the home of Mrs. Hunter and kill her for interfering with his relationship. In his twisted mind, he blamed her for Louiza's murder, as if she were the one who committed the crime.

Thomas kept to the shadows where he observed groups of people looking for him. When he realized the hunt was on, he began to feel conflicted. He decided to go back to the Fox home. He retraced his steps through the night until he reached the farm. Thomas crept silently to the side of the house and peered inside the window. He saw Louiza's body stretched across the table. He thought to himself she was the most beautiful corpse he had ever seen, with her body so pale and still. He wished he could give her one last kiss. Thomas was startled when people came out of the house. He quickly made his way over to the Fox's spring house where hunkered down unseen.

Once inside, Thomas decided the time had come to end his own life. He imagined himself with Louiza in the afterlife where they would remain united for all time.

He fashioned a cradle out of some cloth to hold the rifle in place, strung it over the rafters, and placed a string on the trigger. He tried to shoot himself, but the gun fell, discharging into his chest nearly hitting his heart.

When he realized the shot was not going to prove fatal, he retrieved a knife from his boot. Enraged, he drew it across his own neck, missing his jugular vein. He collapsed to the floor of the barn. The posse arrived and found him bleeding profusely from his self-inflicted wounds.

Many wanted to lynch Thomas immediately. However, they sent for the doctor instead so he could receive medical attention. The physician assured them he would not survive his injuries and justice would be served. The doctor hastily bandaged his wounds to await the inevitable. Somehow, this stubborn coward would not give up! He fully recovered from his physical trauma, and presented himself healthy enough to stand trial.

Thomas was arraigned on murder charges. He was sent to Belmont County Jail in St. Clairsville, Ohio, until his trial in June.

During the trial, many news agencies described his callous and indifferent attitude during the court proceedings. The local Belmont newspaper reported, "The murderer, Thomas Carr, is about twenty-four years of age, low in stature and strongly built, with a physiognomy that indicates a hard hearted, unrefined, debased nature." In this article they mentioned that through the use of physiognomy, they could determine your personality by the shape of your skull. This is no longer recognized as sound medical science.

Newspapers, near and far, captured the precise details of the trial as the country watched with morbid fascination. It was called the worst murder in the history of our nation. Once the trial commenced, the prosecution expeditiously proved their case.

The jury returned a verdict of premeditated and malicious murder. The moral insanity plea waged by the defense failed easily in light of the strong evidence presented. Thomas Carr was found guilty of murder in the first degree and sentenced to death.

The judge had this to say as he rendered the verdict: "Your unfortunate victim cannot be restored to life by any tears of repentance, or by contrition of heart. The crime you have committed can only be expiated by the judgment of the law. It is: that you be taken from hence to the jail of the county, and that you be safely kept. That on Friday, the 20th day of August, in the year of our Lord one thousand eight hundred and sixty-nine, you be taken to the place of execution, and between the hours of nine o'clock and four o'clock in the afternoon of that day, that you be hanged by the neck until you are dead. May God have mercy on you!"

The execution was originally scheduled for August, but was postponed. The new date was set for March of 1870. During the construction of the gallows, Carr took a calculated interest. He continually asked questions about the design. When the scaffolding was complete, he asked for permission to go see it. He inspected the construction with great precision, climbing all over the structure to check its sturdiness. He performed an impressive display of agility and strength. Once finished, he proclaimed this instrument of death a triumph. He congratulated the sheriff, and was returned to his cell.

Thomas Carr walked calmly to the gallows, where he delivered an impassioned final speech on the dangers of alcohol. On March 24, 1870, at 1:11pm, he became the first and only person to be hanged in Belmont County. He was later buried in an unmarked grave at a nearby church.

Louiza Fox was laid to rest in the Salem Cemetery, in Hendrysburg, Ohio, just across the road from her family church. Today the grave is located in western Belmont County in the Egypt Valley Wildlife Area. Her final resting place is marked with a stone obelisk with the following engraved epithet: "Louiza Catharine, child of John L. & Mary Fox, murdered by Thomas Carr, January 21, 1869, aged 13 years 11 months and 12 days."

The spirit of this poor young girl has been sighted near her grave since the time of her death. Her specter has also been reported wandering throughout the cemetery. Many have experienced the ghost of Louiza haunting the scene of her tragic death; her apparition suddenly appearing as people stop to pay their respects at the marker memorializing the murder.

It is said the ghost of Thomas Carr has been seen at the sight of the gruesome murder as well. He has been witnessed roaming the nearby fields. The Methodist Cemetery in St. Clairsville, where it is rumored Carr is buried, has had its own unique haunted tales to tell.

Perhaps the restless spirits of Louiza Fox and Thomas Carr may be destined to roam this earthly plane throughout eternity. But the hope is the two shall never meet again - in this world, or the next. It was a gruesome homicide that rocked the small community of Belmont County and shocked an entire nation. An innocent young life was torn from this world all for the sake of love.

Theresa Argie & Cathi Weber

MAJESTIC LOVE

Victoria And Albert

No book about love and ghosts would be complete without the saga of Queen Victoria and Prince Albert. Their story is one of the world's greatest tales of devotion beyond death. The English queen is known for being the longest reigning female ruler in history, surpassed only recently by Queen Elizabeth II, her great-great-granddaughter. Victoria, last monarch from the House of Hanover, took the crown at the tender age of eighteen during a time of great social and technological changes. England and America embraced the age named for the Queen - the Victorian Era. It was a time of complex ideologies, wavering class distinction, and stringent social behaviors. Standing only 4' 11" tall, Victoria was small in stature but had an enormous presence. She was stubborn, quick tempered, and a political force to be reckoned with.

Many British subjects were fed up with the overindulgence and lavish spending habits of King William and his brothers. They longed for a new ruler who would bring about much needed change. The new young queen would take those duties seriously. First and foremost, she was to keep the royal bloodline by marrying appropriately and producing an heir. Wearing the crown was a God-given right preserved through careful political and strategic maneuvers. The royal power and legitimacy was passed down through the family from one generation to the next. This meant sometimes marriage was between relatives - cousins, possibly even first cousins. Although today we would consider that incest, it was commonplace and widely accepted during this period of time.

Marriage for the royals was more of a business arrangement than an affair of the heart. Luckily for young Queen Victoria, her semi-arranged marriage became one of history's greatest love stories. For Victoria and Albert it was true love, passionate love, and a devotion that not even death could hinder. Their epic tale began in nineteenth century England.

Alexandrina "Victoria" was born on May 24, 1819. She lived in a very confined atmosphere at Kensington Palace. Her father, Prince Edward, Duke of Kent and Strathearn, passed away when she was very young, less than a year old. The most influential people in Victoria's formative years were her mother, Princess Marie Luise Victoria of Saxe-Coburg-Saalfeld, and a man named Sir John Conroy. Conroy, advisor to the princess, was eager to control the power of the throne. The tensions between Conroy, the princess, and the king, led to young Victoria's sequestered life at Kensington.

Victoria's childhood was no doubt a lonely one. She was always under the close supervision of her dowager mother. To avoid unwanted outside influences, Victoria was kept away from other children as much as possible. She had few friends, almost no privacy, and little time for herself. Her days were spent in a rigorous atmosphere of discipline and learning. Victoria dreamed of the day she would be free from the shackles of her overbearing mother and her manipulative advisor, John Conroy.

Victoria was actually 5th in line for the crown, so becoming queen seemed a longshot with little realistic chance of coming to pass. Fate and circumstance fortuitously intervened on her behalf. The sitting monarch, King William had no sons. His brothers had no surviving legitimate male heirs. Although unlikely, it was Victoria who would eventually become Queen of England, Ireland, and the Empress of India. She left an indelible mark on British and world history, and is credited with having a notable influence on people from Europe to the Americas.

The brief and unexpected courtship of Victoria and Albert began when the future queen was seventeen. Her uncle, King Leopold of Belgium, introduced the couple with the desire that they eventually wed. Albert, Prince of Saxe-Coburg, was a German, and not the first choice of consort to those close to Victoria. Her other uncle, King William IV, had Prince Alexander of the Netherlands in mind for his feisty niece. Victoria didn't care for Alexander. He was, in her words, "very plain" and not particularly interesting. Albert, however, was more physically attractive with features she found extremely desirable.

Victoria and Albert first met in person in May of 1836. According to the future queen's letter to her match-making uncle, "he possesses every quality that could be desired to render me perfectly happy." In other words, Victoria was enamored. It was love (or maybe lust) at first sight. She wanted Albert as her husband, her partner. She didn't have long to wait.

King William died on June 20, 1837. With no surviving male heirs in the family eligible to lead, the teenage Victoria ascended the throne, taking her place as the head of the British Royal monarchy. It was a place she would hold for more than sixty years.

Although it was obvious to everyone that Victoria had her sights set on Prince Albert, she did not rush into marriage. They had met only once, but another meeting was in the works. On Albert's second visit, the relationship progressed swiftly. This was more than just a political maneuver; the prince was equally smitten with the young queen. Victoria asked Albert to marry her within days of his arrival. Albert happily accepted her proposal. The two married on February 10, 1840.

Most of what is known about Queen Victoria and Prince Albert's personal life comes from Victoria's diary. Some historians believe that certain details have been whitewashed to paint the queen in a more favorable light. Family members may have removed anything they believed to be controversial or damaging to her royal reputation. Although this is certainly possible, Victoria's written words are generally accepted at face value. Maybe the world has chosen to accept the romanticized legend of her life because it makes for a better story. Regardless, there is no version of Victoria's saga that portrays her as an absolute angel. Instead, she often comes across as an ill-tempered, grudge holding, domineering woman. But she was also highly respected and adored by her subjects. She was, in every sense, a woman with emotional and physical needs, including a healthy sexual appetite. Victoria and Albert's love life would make a true Victorian Era woman blush!

Albert's official designation was "Prince Consort," not king, as the royal title befell only the men in the bloodline. But Albert's influence on the queen was undeniable. At first, Albert had only a marginal effect on her rule. But with the continual successions of pregnancies keeping her physically and mentally compromised, Albert's new role was more defined. He grew to be a significant and essential, albeit largely uncredited, powerhouse behind the throne.

Victoria's main objective was to be an effective royal leader of the British kingdom. She cared little for popular opinion and wanted only what she believed to be best for her country.

During Victoria's reign, the monarchy shifted to more of a figurehead than a true ruling political power. Albert persuaded his queen to lean more on Parliament for the needs of the nation, which she did with some reluctance. Victoria was heavily influenced by her husband's advice. She not only loved Albert, but she respected his intellect and ideas. He was a confidant and a sounding board for affairs of the state

Victoria and Albert had a robust and passionate relationship. Victoria's diaries   are   explicit   when describing   the   couples   wedding   night.   That enthusiasm continued long past the honeymoon phase. Not surprisingly, Victoria became pregnant within weeks of being married. Over their twenty- one year marriage, the royal couple produced four boys and five girls. Some parents would be over the moon with delight, but not Victoria. She had little affection for children, including her own. Albert had may have had similar feelings, although at times he showed genuine love for his growing brood.

It could be that the royal couple had no positive role models of what good parents should be. Their own parents were cold and showed them no real love or tenderness. Victoria and Albert simply had no frame of reference. The fact that they had so many children was a result of their active sex life, not a burning desire to be parents. Victoria had a particular dislike for babies and abhorred the idea of breastfeeding. She wrote in her diary shockingly harsh things about children. "An ugly baby is a very nasty object..." Victoria managed to give birth to nine of these so called "nasty objects" over a span of seventeen years.

Victoria wasn't completely heartless. She knew the importance of having a healthy male heir. Her daughter, Victoria (called Vicky), was born nine months after she and Albert wed. Her second child, Albert Edward (called Bertie) was born less than a year later. Bertie was to be the heir to the throne. He would become King Edward VII. Seven more children followed.

Many of Albert and Victoria's nine children went on to marry others in key political positions, keeping "royal" in the bloodline. Victoria is often called the "grandmother of Europe" because of this practice. Her daughter Vicky married a German, and eventually gave birth to Emperor Kaiser Wilhelm II. Her granddaughter, also named Victoria, married the last Tzar of Prussia, Emperor Nicholas II. The legacy of Queen Victoria and Prince Albert was set.

Queen Victoria's life took a dark turn on December 14, 1861 when her beloved Albert, 42, succumbed to illness and died. Typhoid fever was thought to be the culprit, although modern historians hint at other possible causes. Some think it may have been a form of cancer, although new research hints at Crohn's disease. Whatever the cause, Prince Albert's death was a devastating blow to the queen, a calamity from which she never fully recovered. The loss of Albert sent Victoria into a state of mourning that lasted the remainder of her life.

Queen Victoria was utterly and completely lost without Albert. Her loneliness and grief were all consuming. She defined what was to be the new standard of mourning for generations of Europeans and Americans. Victoria chose to don only black as an outward symbol of her sorrow. She locked herself away in her palace of pain and was not seen publicly for three years. Her subjects developed a moniker for their monarch, calling Victoria the "widow of Windsor."

In 2011, a previously undiscovered letter written by Queen Victoria to military leader Viscount Gough was acquired for auction. It illustrates the unrelenting depths of her despair. The Viscount, a man outside of the royal family, had suffered the death of his own cherished wife. Victoria reached out to express her condolences. She conveyed emotions of both sympathy and envy.

> *"Irreparable as his loss is how blessed to have lived together until the evening of their lives with the comfort and hope of the separation being a short one."*

Victoria's haunting words written in March of 1863, more than a year after Albert's death, made clear that she longed to be reunited with her love. She never fully recovered from her loss and lived the next four decades in a state of continual melancholy. The queen used her time to search for ways to be close to Albert, even if only in spirit.

Any morsel of humor and amusement was buried deep within her wounded soul. To live without Albert was a monumental task for which she was ill prepared. But as queen, she knew she must go on. It was her duty, her moral obligation, to be the Victoria that England needed. Her subjects gave her strength, as did her continuing relationship with Albert. Her husband may have been dead, but his spirit was very much alive. Victoria's devotion was unwavering.

During this time, England was embracing the movement known as Spiritualism - the belief that the living can communicate with the dead. It was popular with both commoners and aristocrats. The Fox sisters from Hydesville, New York, are credited for bringing this new type of religion to the public with their displays of supernatural strangeness. Maggie Fox was only

14 and her sister Kate 11, when in March of 1848, their mundane world exploded into something that would forever change the way people look at death. Unexplained noises and knocks were said to emanate from the spirit of a man murdered in their family home. The sisters could seemingly interact with this ghost, as well as many others, on command.

Mediumship came to the forefront of popular culture. Seances and table tipping sessions became a fashionable pastime for people from all walks of life, including the wealthy and famous. In the United States, those suffering the loss of loved ones during the Civil War flocked to psychics with a fervor. The "Victorians" took their cues from the English queen, who herself was looking to the supernatural for answers.

There are historians who believe Queen Victoria held seances in her palace home. She was desperate to talk to her dead husband. Victoria had entertained the idea of mediums throughout her reign, and there were a couple that she trusted and believed in. One was a teenage boy named Robert James Lees. The thirteen-year-old supposedly contacted the spirit of Prince Albert during a seance. Word of this communication got back to the queen. Victoria was curious but cautious. She sent some trusted subjects from her court to investigate the medium. They went incognito, not revealing their true identities. Lees could see through their deception and, through the spirit of Albert, conveyed very private information. The queen was convinced at the legitimacy of the young boy's talent. She sent for Lees to join her at Buckingham Palace for a private audience.

It is said by relatives of the Lees family that numerous seances were held at request of Queen Victoria. During these communication sessions, Prince Albert "spoke" to his wife with messages from beyond the grave. According to witnesses, it was Albert's actual voice that came through the teenager. The queen believed Lees was truly a conduit for her husband's spirit. She asked Lees to move in, to be her resident spiritual medium. This would give her access to Albert whenever she needed it.

For whatever reason, Lees turned down the request but offered Victoria an alternative. There was another who could channel the spirit of Albert and therefore continue to advise her from the afterlife. He was a hunting guide named John Brown. As a boy, Brown assisted the prince during his hunting trips. If Albert trusted Brown, then Victoria was to do the same. Much to the shock of those around her, Brown became an integral part of Queen Victoria's life, stirring up all sorts of juicy rumors along the way.

According to some occult historians and author J. H. Brennan, John Brown was more than a companion to the queen; he was her personal medium. Through Brown, Victoria could speak and consult with Albert whenever she wished. Rumors of diaries kept by both Brown and Queen Victoria were said to contain detailed accounts of many seances. Unfortunately, none remain in existence today. We have only the word of those who read them and those who sought to keep them from being read. But the idea adds intrigue to Victoria's relationship with Brown.

John Brown was not the sort of man one would expect to keep company of a royal English queen. He was crass, unrefined, and talked to the monarch in a way that many considered disrespectful and uncouth. The physically imposing Brown was also much younger than the queen. His paranormal powers may be questionable as were his true intentions, but it is hard to deny that he was the catalyst for change the grieving widow needed more than anything. Brown help Victoria ease out of her state of mourning and get back into daily life. The queen was invigorated, but why? Was it because she now believed John Brown was the physical embodiment of Prince Albert?

John Brown managed to do what few others could. He developed a close, personal relationship with the monarch. His influence was undeniable. He brought the hermit queen back into the public eye. She took great pleasure in his friendship and they remained close until her death.

Queen Victoria passed away on January 22, 1901. She finally joined her husband in death, reunited as lovers in the afterworld. Her wish granted, the queen could now rest in peace...or could she? It seems the queen may not have been so eager to leave her castle after all.

People have reported strange, unexplainable happenings at Buckingham Palace for centuries. Ghosts of past residents have roamed the gilded halls long after their bodily death. The essence of the dead remain entombed in the castle's foundation and seek to be remembered by the living. Even before Queen Victoria took the throne, the royal residence was said to be haunted by restless souls. Victoria's penchant for seances may have opened the door to increased paranormal activity.

Attempting communication with the other side is often enough to keep the channels open. Victoria's intense longing to hear from Albert may have been a powerful link that remains to this day. Her grief may have manifested into something irresistible to the spirits. The layers of history in such places is undeniable. Joy, ecstasy, sadness, anguish, fear - emotions with the power to transcend the physical world have primed the stone walls for an eternity of hauntings.

Windsor Palace, Buckingham Palace, Osborne House, the Tower of London - these famous British landmarks are said to be teeming with paranormal activity. The spirit of Queen Victoria is not alone in her visitations. Several other royals join her as resident ghosts. King Henry VIII is a popular spirit, along with several of his wives. Queen Catherine Howard, imprisoned for adultery, momentarily escaped her confines in a desperate attempt to reach the king and beg for mercy. Her heartfelt pleas fell on deaf ears. She was beheaded, just as her cousin Anne Boleyn was before her.

Both queens haunt the royal residences. Catherine Howard terrifies visitors as her ghostly apparition runs screaming through the castle corridors. A headless woman in royal garb frequents the place of execution, as well as the infamous Tower of London. The tower itself is a hotbed of paranormal activity, dating back hundreds of years before Queen Victoria ever graced the palace grounds.

Strange ethereal beings glide effortlessly throughout the buildings, defying physics and terrifying visitors and staff. The restless spirits of prisoners wander aimlessly throughout the dark, dank dungeon of the famous bloody tower. Their tortured souls seek solace from the torment that doomed them in life. The gardens and grounds surrounding many of the royal homes are frequented by ghosts of those who lived there, as well those who met their death at the edge of the executioner's axe.

But it is Queen Victoria and Prince Albert who are spotted most often. Their connection to these places, as well as their unbreakable bond of love, are like supernatural magnets. Queen Victoria is said to keep a watchful eye on her royal residences, always critical of any changes made to the grounds or interior. Grand gardens built in honor of Prince Albert are kept in order, less the spirit of the feisty queen express her displeasure. A famous story told by groundskeepers at Windsor Palace recounts Victoria's deep connection to the property and her husband.

Edward VIII was the great-grandson of Victoria and Albert. After the death of his father, George V, he was next in line to be king. Less than a year into his reign, he abdicated. He did it for his lover, Wallis Simpson, an American divorcee. He desperately wanted to marry Simpson, and proposed shortly after taking his place as head of the monarchy. But this was against royal protocol. The public scandal made headlines all over the world. England was shocked when the love-struck king gave up his crown for a chance at true happiness.

Maybe it was for the best. It seems Victoria was not a fan of the flamboyant, twice-married Simpson, and was "not amused" at her attempts to make changes to the royal residence. Simpson apparently had her own ideas for the royal gardens. She asked that certain spruce trees be removed - trees Victoria planted in memory of Prince Albert. Although long dead, the cantankerous queen would not stand for such a travesty! Her angry ghost terrorized the palace gardeners, moaning and flagellating wildly, chasing away anyone attempting to remove the trees. Many who believe in ghosts feel Victoria's spirit would have made Wallis Simpson a target of her rage had she spent any real amount of time at Windsor Palace!

It's no wonder that in a place where true love lingers, hauntings are part of the tapestry. So much emotion, both good and bad, have imprinted on the grounds. One should expect to find ghosts in a place and time where the paranormal was fully expected and accepted. Victoria and Albert, a queen and her consort, remain in perpetuity, locked in an eternal embrace of love beyond the grave.

OBSESSIVE LOVE

The Deadly Deeds Of Ceely Rose

You may have heard the song, "Pleasant Valley Sunday" written by Carole King and Gerry Goffin. It was recorded by The Monkees and became one of their most successful singles. The aptly named song is considered a social commentary about life in an idyllic place, perhaps a state of mind, called Pleasant Valley. It sings about life in a small town where neatly kept yards and friendly neighbors abound; a place where life seems like an eternal holiday and the smell of smoking charcoal briquettes, ready for a barbecue, fill the air. Some of the lyrics of the song speak to this; *"Creature comfort goals, they only numb my soul, and make it hard for me to see, thoughts all seem to stray to places far away, I need a change of scenery."* It is too bad that the subject of our next story never had the opportunity to heed the words of the song and search for a change of scenery.

Pleasant Valley sits in a rural area of Ohio, situated in Richland County. The countryside is picturesque with rolling hills and small valleys filled with bubbling streams. It is steeped in an agricultural tradition with farms still dotting the landscape. It might be this pastoral setting and a chance to escape the city that first attracted Hollywood actors Lauren Bacall and Humphrey Bogart to Pleasant Valley.

Malabar Farm, in Pleasant Valley, was the home of author Louis Bromfield, who was a personal friend of Bogie and Bacall. The Hollywood couple chose the Bromfield farmhouse as the location for their legendary wedding in 1945. Perhaps they didn't realize the dark history of the property - that a triple murder occurred just minutes away. In fact, it's said that this story of sinister evil may have inspired Bromfield to write the book Pleasant Valley. It's hard to envision that a crime of misdirected passion committed well over a century ago could still haunt a community that appears so peaceful and unspoiled.

The Rose family moved to Pleasant Valley in 1880 when David Rose became the owner of the local Schrack Mill. He and his wife, Rebecca, moved into an indistinct clapboard farmhouse situated right across Switzer's creek from the mill.

Their adult son, Walter, moved with them. He intended to work with his father. When David Rose became the miller, he was responsible for grinding all the grain for the close-knit community of farmers in Pleasant Valley. This position lasted for the next sixteen years. They also brought with them their seven-year-old daughter, Celia Frances. They called her Ceely. So, the Rose family of four began their new life in Pleasant Valley.

Ceely was born mentally challenged. She was retained several grades while in elementary school and her learning disabilities demanded constant attention. By the time she was fourteen years old, Ceely was twice the age and size of her classmates. She decided to stop going to school. She was a simple person with a severe stutter. As Ceely grew, she had very few friends. She was often the object of ridicule by not only other children, but also by the adults in town. Ceely's mother worked hard to help her. She patiently tried to teach her to perform simple tasks around the home. However, most of these lessons ended in frustration. The young girl had little ability to master household chores. Ceely was content to spend her time reading the Bible, doing embroidery, playing with her dollhouses, and attending Sunday School.

Even though Ceely remained intellectually immature, her body matured in the regular fashion. By the age of twenty-three she became aware of boys. The family lived in the center of a busy farming community. Ceely spent hours standing at the fence gazing out at her neighbor's field, admiring the young farmhands as they went about their business. She occupied her days hiding behind rocks or in the tree line by the side of the road. Safely concealed, she could observe people without them being aware of her presence. Her reputation for being mean at times led most people to avoid contact with this strange girl. On occasion, Ceely was invited to parties but mostly chose to stay home. No one seemed to take notice of this odd young woman who quietly daydreamed of romance and marriage.

As Ceely spent her hours observing the townsfolk, she became more emotionally distant from her family. She had plenty of time to pursue her own interests. One day the neighbor's seventeen-year-old son, Guy Berry, caught Ceely's eye. The Rose and Berry families did not have a close relationship. It was known around town that the families would not acknowledge one another when passing in public. Ceely, on the other hand, sought out ways to greet Guy each day. She felt she had found the one true love of her life, and reached out to him whenever she could. She spent hours watching him work on his family's plot of land, talking with him every chance she got. Guy wasn't repulsed by his curious neighbor's adoration, although he was surprised. He listened courteously as Ceely openly and brazenly flirted with him. This led Ceely to imagine their courtship proceeding well.

One afternoon, she declared that she and Guy should be married. After this unexpected turn of events, Guy began avoiding her at all costs. This didn't matter to Ceely, and she told anyone who would listen that she and Guy were getting married.

It was then Guy decided he had enough of Ceely's attention. He went to his father and told him the whole story. He pleaded for his father's help. Guy was adamant that Ceely's obsession with him must stop immediately. He told his father that he intended to leave home unless an end was put to this whole unintentional entanglement.

Guy's father, George Berry, approached Ceely's father. Together they had an honest and open conversation about this affair of the heart that was obviously one-sided. When Mr. Berry presented his case to Mr. Rose, he did not fully blame Ceely for her infatuation, but urgently insisted it was time to put an end to it. Mr. Rose promised to talk to his daughter. He reassured Mr. Berry that Ceely would no longer bother his son.

Both men left the conversation feeling confident Ceely's infatuation would end. Mr. Rose was apprehensive as he prepared to confront Ceely. He'd never before had a stern conversation with his simple daughter. He reprimanded Ceely severely and she promised she would stop harassing Guy. She begged her father not to tell her mother. He acquiesced and they did not speak of it again.

Eventually Mrs. Rose and Walter found out about the situation with Guy. They criticized Ceely for her indiscretion and treatment of the Berry boy. Soon her life at home became unbearable. She could no longer interact with the object of her affection. Ceely was kept isolated so her family could closely monitor her actions.

The constant nagging by her family members opened a deep wound that festered unchecked in Ceely's heart. After a few displays of open rebellion, Ceely eventually became quiet and withdrawn. She had arrived at some distorted conclusion that her family was the only barrier between her and her true love. Ceely was convinced if she removed this obstacle she would be free to marry Guy. In her delusion, she plotted to erase her father, mother and brother from the equation as quickly as possible.

Ceely gave the outward appearance of becoming helpful and courteous to her family once more; she was the diligent and dutiful daughter. She was helpful around the kitchen, especially at meal time. One morning, Ceely insisted on preparing the family's breakfast of cottage cheese. She gave her father and brother generous portions and her mother a smaller serving. Mr. Rose and Walter ate heartily while Mrs. Rose only picked at her breakfast. Ceely ate none of the cottage cheese that morning. After her family finished the meal, she cleaned up around the kitchen, placing the leftover cottage cheese on a plate. Later in the day, she threw it out into the yard.

Shortly after breakfast, her father suddenly became sick and began to vomit violently. The family was concerned and sent Walter for the doctor. On his way to retrieve the physician, Walter became ill as well. Neighbors found him lying in the road and brought him back to the house. The town physicians were summoned to the Rose residence, where they speculated that poison was behind this sudden illness. Ceely's mother also became sick that evening, but her symptoms were mild and not nearly as extreme. Her father, however, succumbed to his symptoms after six agonizing days. Walter followed his father to the grave within five days. After two weeks, Ceely's mother seemed to be on the mend. Since she was feeling better, she asked her caring and attentive daughter if she might have some milk and bread. Suddenly she worsened. Rebecca Rose died the next day. Still, not much attention was paid the intellectually challenged daughter of now deceased David and Rebecca Rose.

Before her death, Mrs. Rose was questioned by authorities regarding the fatal breakfast she shared with her family. She adamantly dismissed the idea that poison could have found its way into their food. Many concluded she was trying to protect her daughter. At first, Ceely denied her role in preparing breakfast the morning in question, but later admitted she had helped. Once she realized suspicion had been cast her way, Ceely wholly retracted her admission stating she had nothing to do with the meal that morning.

After the death of her family, Ceely was not immediately charged. She stayed with the few neighbors who supported her and believed her innocent. The rest of the valley thought otherwise. Early in the investigation, an autopsy on David Rose was performed. Traces of arsenic were found in the lining of David's stomach. The poison was believed to originate from a product called "Rough on Rats," commonly used by many households in that era. This was corroborated by several physicians. Criminal proceedings against Ceely Rose were initiated. The prosecutor decided that in the interest of justice and a speedy trial, he wanted Ceely to confess.

He sought out the one person who had befriended her through the years; Theresa Davis, considered a trusted childhood friend of Ceely. Theresa was asked for her help in extricating a confession. She privately begged Ceely to confess. Ceely ended up telling Theresa everything.

Ceely went on to disclose every minute detail of the devious plot to murder her family. She found some recently purchased rat poison in the pantry. After putting a liberal pinch in the pepper mill, she sprinkled it on the cottage cheese before serving her family. She also revealed a hen and seven chicks died after she threw the leftover cottage cheese out into the yard. In the weeks that followed, Ceely dutifully tended to her mother. One day she overheard the doctor tell Mrs. Rose that she was recovering nicely. Ceely then tainted her mother's glass of milk with the poison pepper to finish her off. She recalled this worked very well, for Mrs. Rose began vomiting almost immediately after consuming the milk.

Celia Frances Rose was arrested and charged with the murder of her family. She was held by a grand jury without bond pending her trial. During her first hearing, Ceely would alternate between a teary-eyed breakdown and unabashed laughter. Her unstable mental state became obvious, and was highlighted as an important piece of evidence during the trial. The prosecution was confident they had a strong case. Ceely was found not guilty by reason of insanity for the murders of her three family members.

In 1898, she was remanded to the Toledo State Mental Hospital to serve her lifelong sentence. In 1915, Ceely was moved to the brand-new Lima State Hospital for the Criminally Insane. She died there in 1934 and is buried in the Lima State Hospital Cemetery.

Over the years, paranormal activity has been reported originating from the family home of Ceely Rose. This estate exists today at Malabar Farm, an Ohio state park dedicated to the preservation and research of rural agriculture. The house sits vacant, but the curious onlooker has seen the shadow of a young woman pass by an upstairs window, peeking from behind a curtain. The location of the window is the bedroom once occupied by Ceely Rose.

People have claimed to observe Ceely late at night wandering the grounds of her old home. Perhaps she's looking to encounter Guy Berry once again? Malabar Farm and the Bromfield Estate are both said to have their own share of strange happenings. It seems entire grounds of this state park are filled with ghost stories - from the library of the big house to the ladies' public restroom!

Ohio author and playwright, Mark Jordan, was so touched by the true story of Ceely Rose he wrote a play about it. Actors brought Ceely's story to life in the barn at Malabar Farm. Beginning in 2003, the play ran intermittently for over a decade. This popular production, simply called "Ceely," played for sold out crowds during its run. Mr. Jordan reported many technical malfunctions with the lighting and sound that could not be easily explained during production. Maintenance experts could not understand these mechanical failures. Could these unusual occurrences be the spirit of Ceely Rose providing playful interference?

Many supernatural experiences have been reported in the barn by visitors or those attending a performance. One reason given for the haunting is said to be the use of reclaimed wood beams from the old Schrack Mill - the mill that held so much meaning to the Rose family. Ethereal girlish giggles have been heard inside the darkened building.

Phantom footsteps emanate from all corners of the empty structure. Doors will open slowly and suddenly bang shut without explanation. Cameras and cellphones are known to mysteriously malfunction. A nearby restroom has ladies running in fear. It is said the last stall has a malevolent spirit that will be sure to let you know you're not welcome there. Even the walls can talk! Banging and rapping sounds coming from the walls in the bathroom have been reported. Women tend to sense the presence of something unseen while in this building, leaving them with an eerie feeling. The list of odd occurrences is long at this location.

Many ghostly tales have come from the home of Louis Bromfield, both from those who work there and those who have visited. The lights inside the house have a tendency to turn off and on by themselves. Visitors have taken photos that show traces of ghostly figures and transparent apparitions. Some have felt the sensation of otherworldly fingers lightly touching their arm. Items seem to move of their own volition. Phantom faces have appeared in the windows of the big house after hours.

Some suggest it's Louis Bromfield, or even Ceely Rose.

Ceely Rose committed murder in the name of love. One has to wonder, was she really insane, or truly diabolical? As we read her story, it's obvious we may never know who the true Ceely was. We may have to rely on only her ghost to tell the twisted tale. It seems Ceely has no intentions of moving on and leaving behind her beloved Guy.

MORBID LOVE

The Madness Of Count Carl Von Cosel

One of the most disturbing tales of love beyond death is the gruesome story of Carl von Cosel. He was born Karl Tanzler on February 8, 1877, in Dresden, Germany. He changed his name to the former later in life. For the purposes of our story, we will refer to him as Carl von Cosel.

Von Cosel was educated, curious, driven, and by all accounts delusional. His passion for invention fueled his thirst for knowledge beyond what Germany could offer. He was destined for better things. Although a man of science, von Cosel had strong beliefs in the supernatural. To him, the two were inseparable. In his diary (**The Secret of Elena's Tomb** by Carl von Cosel), he details several episodes of the paranormal throughout his life. Strange unearthly noises, ghostly apparitions, and violent poltergeist activity often interrupted his work.

Paranormal incidents began when he was young. At the tender age of twelve, von Cosel had an eerie encounter with a supernatural being. This was far more than a garden-variety haunting; it was a prophetic vision with a ghostly entity. A spectral woman in white spoke in detail of his destiny and revealed the thinly veiled face of his future bride. The information foretold on that day sent him on a bizarre journey; a crash course into madness.

The mysteries of the supernatural were an accepted part of von Cosel's life. As a child, he learned of a haunted castle, Villa Cosel, located not far from his home. The ghostly tale led to his eventual name change from Karl Tanzler to Carl von Cosel.

According to legend, Villa Cosel was once Napoleon Bonaparte's headquarters. The castle was inhabited by a female apparition known as The White Lady. She was the ghost of Countess Anna Cosel, a beautiful woman in line to marry Augustus the Strong, the future King of Poland.

Countess Anna never became queen. She fell out of favor when a jealous courtesan whispered unseemly rumors in the king's ear. The countess was abruptly removed from the king's court and exiled to a dreary life of solitude. She remained locked away in the castle until her death in 1765. During this time, the countess indulged her insatiable appetite for alchemy. She turned her castle prison into a giant experimental laboratory.

Carl von Cosel believed he was a direct descendant of Countess Anna Cosel. They were connected by blood and ambition. Her spirit was his guide. She instilled in him a love of science and experimentation, while strengthening his belief in the occult .The White Lady appeared to von Cosel many times over the course of his life. In his diary, von Cosel described prophetic messages from the spirit of Countess Anna. She often spoke of his beloved, his bride to be. She was a young dark-haired woman with ebony curls that framed her delicate face. Von Cosel believed he would one day find this woman. Nothing on Earth could ever keep them apart.

While waiting for his true love, von Cosel married another; a German woman named Doris. She was a devoted wife, but not the one foretold by the ghostly countess. The couple had two daughters, Crysta and Aeysha. But marital vows and fatherly responsibility didn't fulfill the restless scientist.

Not content with his life in Germany, von Cosel left Europe and his family in 1926. In his mind, he was on an epic journey much like Odysseus in **The Odyssey**. He spent time in various countries with an array of jobs, creating several different personas and identities during his travels. He wrote about incredible adventures while abroad. He posed as a doctor, an inventor, and a count. The validity of his writings is questionable, likely more romanticized than reality.

Von Cosel was always tinkering with mechanical inventions.He made preposterous claims about his engineering abilities. One such claim was about a device called an "airship." It was a wingless plane that could transport someone anywhere in the universe. It may have been a rudimentary rocket of some sort, powered by insanity and imagination.

Von Cosel spent time in Cuba, among other places, before reaching his final destination, Florida. His long-suffering wife, Doris, and their two daughters joined him in the United States in 1927. Not long after their arrival, von Cosel walked out on them again. This time he traveled south to Key West.

Once von Cosel arrived in Key West, he immediately began to reinvent himself. This is when he changed his name from Karl Tanzler to Carl von Cosel - "Count" Carl von Cosel. He claimed to be a doctor of German royalty, ancestor of Countess Anna Cosel. Regardless of his true legal name, his discernible medical background made him very employable.

During this time, tuberculosis was ravaging the country at an epidemic rate. The multitudes of those suffering from the incurable disease overwhelmed medical resources. Von Cosel found a job at Marine Hospital as an attendant and an X-ray technician. He worked in the pathology lab reviewing x-rays, looking for evidence of hardy consumption. He was often mistaken for a physician, a mistake he used to his advantage.

Von Cosel's life changed forever the day a young dark-haired woman walked into his lab. Twenty-one-year-old Elena Milagro Hoyos came to the hospital with the tell-tale signs of tuberculosis. She was frail and sickly, yet stunningly beautiful. The count was spellbound.

Von Cosel immediately recognized Elena as his beloved. She was the woman from his visions. Her hair, her eyes, her essence - there was no doubt in his mind. As the White Lady foretold, she was the one he'd waited for all these years. Elena was quiet, shy, and terrified at her prognosis. She had no idea what forbidden desires stirred in the heart of her new doctor. Tuberculosis wasn't the darkest part of her future. Elena's fate would be something unimaginable, something far worse than death.

Von Cosel was overjoyed and utterly devastated at the same time. He had found his beloved, but she was stricken with a terrible sickness that was most certainly a death sentence. He could not bear the thought of finding her only to lose her so soon. It was obvious that Elena was unaware of her destiny with von Cosel. This fact was sure to reveal itself in time, although time was slipping away.

Von Cosel faced several obstacles with Elena. For one, she was already married. Elena was still in love with her husband, Luis. They had only been married a short time but had already encountered much tragedy. Elena desperately wanted children but her first pregnancy ended in a miscarriage. Now, Elena was sick with a highly contagious and incurable disease. Her husband wasn't the "in sickness and in health" type; he couldn't handle the diagnosis. Luis abandoned Elena shortly after she became ill. He preferred to 'live to love another" than to die alongside his sick wife.

The devious von Cosel took great steps to earn Elena and her family's trust. They were desperate and von Cosel capitalized on their worst fears. He convinced them of his medical prowess and claimed he was her only hope. He was determined to save her and would let no treatment go untried. Elena's parents welcomed the attention from this older, more experienced German-born doctor. To the Hoyos family, this was the miracle they prayed for. Elena's best chance at survival was under the care of this physician; the man they knew as Count von Cosel.

Von Cosel came to their home to treat Elena, who grew sicker by the day. The charming count never showed up empty-handed. He brought gifts of wine and fruit along with his medical supplies. He bought Elena a new bed when her old one broke, complete with the finest of linens. He even made presents of jewelry and other pretty baubles. Von Cosel claimed he did these things in order to make his patient smile, because morale was just as important as medicine. The Hoyos family thought he was an angel. They couldn't believe their fortune in finding this amazing doctor to treat their Elena.

Von Cosel was on a mission to find a cure. He was willing to try anything, no matter how unconventional. He invented an electroshock box used to stimulate the healing process. The device sent a series of electric impulses throughout Elena's body. The shock therapy ranged from mildly ticklish to abruptly painful, sometimes making Elena cry. Such treatments allowed von Cosel to get physically close to his patient. It was these examinations where von Cosel could freely touch his beloved. He cherished these fleeting moments of physical contact with Elena.

The family grew concerned with this unorthodox treatment. Something about the doctor seemed off. His hands lingered a bit too long when administering examinations. His eyes expressed an intense euphoric gaze. They were unaware of his deep-seated feelings for Elena, but instinct told them the relationship was not normal. The shrewd von Cosel always managed to quell their fears by showering them with expensive gifts and promises of a cure.

Unbeknownst to Elena, von Cosel's madness was growing as rapidly as the tuberculosis in her body. In his mind, everything was falling into place. All the prophecies were coming true. Any sign was taken as confirmation of their inevitable bond. The slightest look or wayward smile became, in von Cosel's twisted mind, something more - a declaration of love. They would one day be wed and live together in matrimonial bliss. In his memoirs, he claimed Elena not only consented to his proposal of marriage, but she initiated it.

As his fantasy grew, Elena slipped further away. The disease was unrelenting. She could no longer stave off the infection that ravished her ever- weakening body. No matter what he tried, von Cosel could no longer slow the inevitable. He watched helplessly as she grew closer and closer to death.

After fighting for months, Elena Milagro Hoyos succumbed to her affliction. She passed away on October 25, 1931. Von Cosel was heartbroken. His love was gone. What was to become of them? Elena was his destiny as foretold to him by the spirit of his ancestor, Countess Anna Cosel. He couldn't accept that this was the end.

The Hoyos family was devastated. Keeping with their faith, the family planned a traditional Catholic burial for Elena. Somehow, von Cosel persuaded the family to let him help with the funeral arrangements. He swayed them into the idea that Elena was worthy of much more than a simple grave. She deserved a very special tomb, one more suited to a princess. She should have a mausoleum.

As a token of his sympathy, he would, of course, pay for this grand above-ground burial chamber. There they would have a place to visit and pay their respects. The family could see no harm in this and agreed to let von Cosel have his way. They never imagined the true intentions of the mad count. There was a horrifying reason behind his generosity. It would be years before his morbid obsession and insidious actions would come to light.

Von Cosel made good on his word to provide a mausoleum for Elena, but this was no ordinary crypt. He designed a final resting place that was anything but final. In a pristine spot in Key West Cemetery, Carl von Cosel erected the tomb of Elena Hoyos. This chamber had a few hidden features known only to himself and the spirit world. He installed a lock for which he held the only key. He would need access to the tomb for the next phase of his unspeakable scheme.

Von Cosel's delusions were deep and unwavering. He believed Elena called to him from the grave. She loved him and begged him to marry her. He visited her nightly, entering the tomb with his key. There, they could be together, alone and away from prying eyes. Being a man of mature age, Von Cosel's visits became more and more physically taxing. He alleviated this problem with another one of his inventions. He had a makeshift telephone installed in Elena's crypt so she could talk to him whenever she desired.

Von Cosel had bigger and more perverse plans. He continued to work at home on one of his airship inventions. When the time was right, he would use it to transport Elena to the stars. He believed the solar radiation could regenerate her physical body. The deranged doctor couldn't sleep. At night, he heard the sweet sound of Elena singing to him from beyond the grave. Her spirit was very much alive, but she was cold and scared. She pleaded with him to save her from the loneliness of the mausoleum. She wanted to come home to their home, the one they would share as husband and wife.

Von Cosel had access to the tomb whenever he wanted, but this didn't satisfy his needs. With the growing physical desires of any man about to marry, von Cosel needed to be with his love. It was time - von Cosel and Elena would be united. The bridegroom made the necessary preparations. He filled his makeshift laboratory with supplies. He had everything needed. Now he had only to bring home his bride.

Under the cover of night and with the blessings of his ancestors, Carl von Cosel set out to steal the body of Elena Hoyos. One moonlit evening, von Cosel made his way to the cemetery with a wagon full of tools and blankets. His heart pounded with audible force.

Von Cosel journeyed through the graveyard with remarkable ease, considering the payload he had in tow. When he arrived at the tomb, he broke open the locks, busted the seal, and worked his way to Elena's coffin. Once opened, he carefully removed her decaying body and placed it in his wagon. The smell of decay filled his nostrils, but he continued his maniacal labor of love. Von Cosel trembled uncontrollably as he wrapped Elena's corpse in the blanket.

In his diary, von Cosel tells a remarkable story born from the depths of his deprived mind. The angels in heaven favored this union. The cemetery spirits lined up to greet them as the wagon passed by. Like guests at a wedding celebration, they sang in joyous unity. They illuminated the path and removed all obstacles that might hinder the couple's journey home.

Once back in his lab, Von Cosel used his medical knowledge to preserve Elena's physical form. Carefully, he washed her body and dressed her in a fine white gown. He used concoctions of oils and waxes on her skin, removed rotting flesh and replaced it with silk and cloth. Perfumes masked the stench of decomposition. Glass eyes replaced the originals. He also made a death mask of her face. To him, Elena was as beautiful as any bride on her wedding night.

Carl von Cosel finally had what he longed for all his life – his one true love. According to von Cosel's diary, Elena wanted them to be together in every way - emotionally and physically. The mad doctor inserted a paper tube into her vaginal canal to make sexual intimacy possible. With Elena's blessing, the couple consummated the marriage. The unholy union went undetected for seven years.

The Hoyos family had no idea that they were paying their respects to an empty tomb. Von Cosel carefully hid his dark secret from the outside world. Eventually, people began to suspect something wasn't right. Von Cosel suddenly stopped visiting Elena's grave. When his pattern changed, people wondered why. At first, some assumed he had simply died, but the truth was far worse. Rumors began to circulate that von Cosel had taken Elena's body from the mausoleum. When Elena's sister heard this, she began an investigation. The Hoyos family had her tomb opened; to their shock and horror, it was empty.

The police were summoned to von Cosel's home where they found the count alive and well. As they questioned the count, they noticed a putrid odor;

something unnatural and alarming. Authorities soon uncovered his diabolical secret. There, in the bedroom where Carl von Cosel slept, lay the morbidly preserved body of Elena Hoyos. She was covered with a wax-like film and dressed in a fine white dress; her glass eyes open as if pleading to be rescued from the nightmare. It was a horrific scene.

This was the most shocking and gruesome discovery ever made in Key West. The world soon learned of von Cosel's grave robbing and deplorable acts of necrophilia. Mortified, the family and people of Key West demanded justice. Von Cosel never wavered in his conviction that he had done no wrong, that Elena wanted to be with him as much as he with her. He believed the marriage was consensual.

Von Cosel truly believed he was the real victim in the affair. He was arrested, taken from his home, and separated from his young wife. Von Cosel was never prosecuted for his actions. The statute of limitations on his crimes grave robbing and abuse of a corpse - had run out and he was released from jail. The publicwas outraged at the actions of von Cosel and lack of punishment he received. Where was decency and justice? After the arrest, the Hoyos family re-interned the body of Elena in a secret location. They hoped this would let her finally rest in peace. Von Cosel would never see his beloved again.

Word of von Cosel's grisly deed rocked the nation. Photographs of Elena's astonishingly well-preserved body circulated all over the country. Curiosity seekers flocked to the Keys hoping to catch a glimpse of the "sleeping beauty." Eventually, von Cosel slipped back into obscurity. In a strange twist of fate, he reunited with Doris, his legal wife, and their daughters. They supported him throughout the trial and in the aftermath of his public shaming.

There were rumors that von Cosel spent years searching for Elena's grave. Then one day he suddenly stopped. Could it be that he finally gave up, or had he found his bride and once again brought her back home? Years later, in July of 1952, Karl Tanzler, aka Count Carl Von Cosel, was found dead at his home in Pasco County, Florida. Officially, he died of natural causes. But there was something strange about the discovery, something no one could prepare for.

Authorities found von Cosel's body nestled in the arms of a makeshift mannequin. The form resembled a young Hispanic woman with long dark hair. He had created the life-size doll using a death mask of Elena. A strange coffin- like structure was also discovered. This was one of von Cosel's "airships." He never gave up on the idea of reanimating his beloved. One day he would send her body deep into the heavens where she would be made whole again.

The ghost of Elena Hoyos is said to haunt Key West to this day. If there was ever a reason for a restless spirit to wander the land, this would be it. She was afflicted with a devastating disease that took her life too soon. She was raped and abused by a madman. She was disinterred, defiled, and then put on display.

The ghost of Count Carl von Cosel, aka Karl Tanzler, also haunts the island paradise. His strong belief in the supernatural makes it likely that he is still pursuing his bride. He searches the graveyards and lonely shores for his beloved Elena. To the people of Key West, he will always be "Mad Count von Cosel: grave robber, necromancer, defiler of the dead."

ANIMAL SPIRITS

"Tails" Of Devotion

Animal spirits hold a profound fascination for many paranormal enthusiasts. By definition, they are "inhuman" because, technically, they are not, nor have ever been "human." That doesn't necessarily mean they are bad, or evil, or demonic. They are just different ghostly entities that originated from a non-human source.

There are thousands of stories about animal spirits circulating the internet. Astonishing tales of ghost dogs, phantom felines, or even haunted horses. Some are quite terrifying. From demonic Hellhounds in search of human souls to devilish black cats that serve an ominous warning of death and doom. Or ghostly soldiers and their trusty steeds haunting the roads of Gettysburg. The examples are endless.

But what about our animal companions? Can they become spirits as well? Of course they can! Their energy can transform and hold tight to this earthly plane. When a beloved pet dies but returns as a ghost, it is a gift from the universe. It gives us another moment, another memory of that animal who was part of our family. What wouldn't you do for one more cuddle or kiss from your best furry friend?

We keep our pets close to us with an eternal leash of love.

Some animals seem to have a connection that's as strong as any force in existence. Love knows no boundaries. It cannot be quelled by death, or time, or even species. Many believe the physical death of one does not break the bond between a pet and its master. The corporeal association may be severed but the emotional kinship remains. The theory is that animals sense the death of their human companions. They exhibit very human-like behavior. They seem to know things beyond the logical limits of their smaller, less complex brains. They have emotions.

Animals can mourn. They can feel loss and sadness. They can even die of a broken heart. Emotions may be the glue that keeps them here with us, even after death. Is it our sorrow or is it theirs? It doesn't seem to matter.

Devoted Dogs

None of God's creatures exhibit the loyalty and devotion that dogs have for their human counterparts. This trait crosses all cultural boundaries. Those who say animals are incapable of love have never heard of these special dogs.

Yukon

Anyone who has a dog knows they can be fiercely loyal and form deep attachments to certain people or places. Our homes become their homes. Our lives and theirs become inseparable. This is the story of a very special dog that haunts a rather unusual venue; more of a second home than anything else.

Yukon, a beautiful brown Labrador, accompanied his master to work nearly every day from the time he was a puppy until his death ten years later. Yukon was a regular fixture at Willoughby Coal, a hardware and contractor supply store in northeast Ohio. As a puppy, the four-footed fluff ball was a welcomed novelty for customers and staff at the historic company. The business grew as did the lovable dog. People looked forward to seeing Yukon's happy tail wagging vigorously whenever they stopped in. He was beloved by everyone, especially the employees and owner of the bustling business. Yukon's job was an ambassador, a mascot of sorts. People couldn't help but smile when seeing the beautiful happy animal.

Inevitably, dogs grow older, just as people do, and Yukon was getting up in years. His fur was not so shiny and his failing eyes were not so bright. He didn't get around as easily anymore. He spent most of his days curled up by the heater, sometimes getting up to greet customers as they came and went. Even as his health declined, the loyal pooch came to work daily with his master.

One wintry afternoon as the staff prepared to go home, Yukon's master noticed he wasn't waiting in his usual spot - a blanket on the floor by the antique pot bellied stove. Everyone looked around for the elderly Lab but he was nowhere to be found. On a whim, someone looked outside and saw canine paw prints in the snow. The prints led from the front door of Willoughby Coal to the railroad tracks about 20 yards away. There, lying in the gravel next to the tracks, was poor Yukon. He'd been hit by a passing train. Yukon was brought back inside Willoughby Coal where he died in his master's arms. It was a sad day for all.

But Yukon never really left.

Store employees reported hearing and seeing the dog regularly after he passed. At first they dismissed the events, chalking it up to grief and overactive imaginations. But the sightings continued. Even today, more than a decade after his death, Yukon's spirit is still active inside Willoughby Coal. And he is not alone.

The ghost of a previous owner, upset about a wrongful death, lingers throughout the three story building. He is joined by the spirit of Zip, an eccentric man with unusual habits who worked there for many years. A phantom female has made her presence known on several occasions, both visually and audibly. Strange shadow figures lurk in darkened corners, manifesting out of the thick brick walls. Even the local police concur something strange is happening inside the iconic building. They've witnessed ghostly faces in the windows and weird light anomalies, even when the business is closed. Willoughby Coal is arguably one of the most haunted locations in Ohio.

The Haunted Housewives have investigated the building well over a hundred times. Its historic significance has made it a favorite local haunt. Paranormal encounters at Willoughby Coal include bizarre light phenomenon, disembodied voices, phantom footsteps, doors that open and close by themselves, and an unprecedented number of EVPs. These events can be incredibly frightening, especially during daylight hours. Who expects to run into a ghost while buying cement or PVC pipe?

Nighttime brings a more malevolent type of paranormal activity, keeping the Haunted Housewives on our toes.

But the ghost of Yukon is our favorite. He doesn't seek to scare anyone away, he's just doing what dogs do; protecting his territory. The loyal canine has found peace and comfort at Willoughby Coal. Long after his tragic death, Yukon has decided to spend his afterlife in the place he loved best with the people who still appreciate his happy gentle spirit.

Hachiko

One of the most well-known examples of animal love and loyalty is the story of Hachiko. Born in Japan in 1923, the dog's unshakable love for his master was legendary. This caught the attention of newspapers and dog lovers all over the world. His story garnered international fame and became the inspiration for several books and movies.

Akitas are a breed known for their fierce loyalty. Hachiko was the epitome of this characteristic. His master, Hidesamuro (sometimes written as Hidesaburo or Eizaburo) Ueno, was a professor of Agriculture at the University of Tokyo. He took the train from the Shibuya station to and from work every day. Hachiko, his faithful dog, was always there at 4 o'clock to greet him. Dog and master continued this meet-and-greet routine for sixteen months like clockwork. Tragedy struck in 1925, when Professor Ueno suffered a fatal brain hemorrhage at work and passed away.

Hachiko, unaware of Ueno's demise, waited as usual at the station platform. Train after train arrived but the professor never disembarked. Eventually, the dog went home but Ueno was not there either. The poor dog would never see his master again.

Eventually Hachiko realized Ueno was not coming home, so he made his way back to the last place they were together - the train station. The loyal Akita waited, but no professor. Confused but undeterred, Hachiko returned to Shibuya the next day. And the next day...and the next. Hachiko did this for nearly ten years.

The dog's hopeless plight was evident. Hachiko was eventually taken in by the professors' assistant, who tried to continue caring for the orphaned animal. Many train regulars took pity on Hachiko and often brought him food or treats. There was a small, but comfortable dog bed set up for him, courtesy of the station managers.

Hachiko never fully accepted another master. People traveled from all over Japan to see the remarkable Akita in person and marvel at his unfettered devotion. Try as they might, no one could persuade Hachiko to alter his course. The loyalty of this remarkable dog became legendary.

Hachiko's journey finally ended in March of 1935. His lifeless body was found on a street near the train station. All of Japan mourned his passing. Animal behaviorists said it was habit, not love that drove the dog to repeat this pattern. Those who witnessed the dog's actions vehemently disagreed.

Hachiko was driven by love and loyalty, an unexplainable bond that defies logic and nature. A beautiful bronze statue of the loyal Akita was placed at the Shibuya Station. It stands as a memorial to the dog who touched the hearts of animal lovers from all over the world. In 2009, Hollywood released a movie inspired by this story, "Hachi: A Dog's Tale," starring Richard Gere.

Capitán

In March of 2006, an Argentinian man named Miguel Guzman passed away unexpectedly. Shortly thereafter, the family dog, Capitán, disappeared from the home. He was a beautiful black and gray German Shepherd mix who was never far from Guzman's side. After his death, the Guzman family was deep in their mourning and preoccupied with funeral arrangements. No one realized the dog was missing from the home until some days later.

The family discovered Capitán in the cemetery while

visiting Guzman's grave. They were very surprised to see the dog, most assumed he had run away. Guzman's son, Damian first noticed Capitán as he approached his father's grave. He was "barking as if he were crying." The bewildered family called to Capitán but he refused to budge. The dog seemed heartbroken and confused.

How Capitán made his way to the cemetery and somehow found Guzman's grave is a mystery.

The family's bewilderment at the sight of Capitán is understandable. Miguel Guzman died in a hospital and was then taken to a mortuary for burial preparation before he was eventually laid to rest in the cemetery. Neither location was near the Guzman house. There is no easy explanation of how the dog found his master's grave.

Capitán reluctantly followed the family home once, but returned to the grave a while later. He always came back to Guzman's grave! The caretakers of the cemetery said Capitán had a familiar routine. Although the dog sometimes wandered the grounds during the day, he always ended up at the same spot by evening. At 6 pm he'd lay down at the foot of the grave as if settling in for the night.

Capitán stayed by his master's final resting place for years. He became a local and then international legend for his extraordinary behavior. Scores of newspapers have photographed the loyal pooch. Alone and resolute, Capitán kept watch over the one person he felt the most connected to in life.

What supernatural sense guided Capitán to his master's final resting place? What mysterious force compelled him to stay? Dozens of eyewitness accounts validate this story but no one can explain it. It shows an unbreakable bond of love between a man and his dog.

Capitán passed away in 2017. After eleven long lonely years, he has finally been reunited with his master.

Greyfriars Bobby

Scotland holds claim to one of the most famous tales of canine loyalty and devotion. The story of Greyfriars Bobby has touched the hearts of thousands of animal lovers for over 150 years. Bobby, the little Skye Terrier with the sad eyes and wiry mane, is immortalized with a statue of his likeness erected in arguably the most haunted graveyard in the world. More than a century and a half after his death, the adorable pup lives on - in books and in films, including a Disney movie released in 1961. There are conflicting versions of this story and questions about its legitimacy, but the heart of the tale remains consistent.

Bobby was a loyal companion to his owner, John Gray. Some say Gray was a gardener turned constable for the Edinburgh Police, others claim he was a shepherd. I tend to believe the constable version and will share the story as such. Part of Gray's duties was to patrol Edinburgh's streets, keeping safe those sleeping silently in the night. No matter the weather, Bobby, his faithful dog, was always at his side. The two made an inseparable pair, vigilantly walking the beat of alleyways and avenues. Gray was happy to have Bobby's company during the dreary midnight rounds he made through the old Scottish neighborhoods.

In February of 1858, Gray succumbed to tuberculosis (or possibly pneumonia). He was buried at Greyfriars Kirkyard, not far from the streets he so diligently safeguarded. Poor Bobby was now alone, lost without his loving friend. It wasn't long before the locals and staff at Greyfriars noticed a ragamuffin stray who looked remarkably like Bobby hanging around near the site of John Gray's burial. The diminutive dog was steadfast and refused to leave the grave of his master. Try as they might to shoo away the terrier, Bobby always came back. Be there rain, or snow, or bitter cold - the ritual continued, even in the most severe, inhospitable conditions.

The locals, with help of the cemetery caretakers, erected a makeshift shelter for the sweet little dog. He had a definite routine. The one o'clock gun was the signal for Bobby to leave for his lunch. Each day at the exact time, he followed a sympathetic friend to a local coffee house or tavern where he was given a welcomed meal. After he had his fill, Bobby returned to the grave, content until the next afternoon. Each day was the same for the little dog. Days turned into weeks, weeks into months, months into years.

Bobby's vigilant and unwavering plight touched the hearts of many visitors to Greyfriars Kirkyard. Scottish law required dog owners to register their pets. Strays were considered a nuisance and often euthanized. In 1867, Bobby was given a license by The Lord Provost of Edinburgh, an act that saved him from being put down. Now legally allowed in the Kirkyard, Bobby was free to come and go as he pleased.

Bobby followed the same heartbreaking routine for fourteen years. No amount of coaxing could get the little dog to abandon his master's final resting place for long. Bobby finally passed away in January of 1872. A bronze statue made in the likeness of the Skye Terrier was placed just inside the entrance of Greyfriars Kirkyard to honor the dog whose "loyalty and devotion be a lesson to us all."

But Bobby's story doesn't end there. In recent years, researchers have questioned the legitimacy of this tale. Indeed, there are widely varying versions and some logically sketchy details. According to the historic timeline, Bobby would have been sixteen when he passed. That in itself seems hard to believe...but not impossible. There are those who believe there was more than one Bobby. The original "Bobby" was replaced at some point in time. This would account for the unusual longevity of the little dog. Some believe the story was a complete hoax or a publicity stunt - perpetuated to drum up business for a local pub (also called Greyfriars Bobby) and bring visitors to the historic cemetery.

And that may be true, at least in part. But animal lovers know the bond between dog and master often defies logic and explanation. We embrace the undeniable fact that a dog can show love and devotion beyond what humans think possible.

Death has not strayed the little dog from his course. Bobby still visits his master's grave! The spirit of the Skye Terrier haunts Greyfriars, faithfully completing his routine. People have spotted a small dog, remarkably similar to Bobby, wandering the graveyard alone. A small shadowy form is seen scurrying in the Kirkyard at night. Caretakers search in vain for what they believe to be a stray, or a local pet that has wandered in by mistake. Some manage to find the mysterious mutt, only to watch him inexplicably vanish right before their eyes. The all-too familiar howl of a distraught dog breaks the silence of the Scottish night. Ear piercing, sorrowful cries echo through the darkened cemetery. The anguish and pain of the lonely dog is palpable. A local Scottish legend states if a full moon falls on Halloween night, the spirit of Greyfriars Bobby will resurrect from his grave in search of a new master.

Even daytime visitors to Greyfriars Kirkyard have eerie encounters with the spirit of Bobby. Many who walk their dogs through the cemetery during daylight hours report frightening activity when close to Bobby's statue. Some dogs bark and growl at an unseen entity. Others cry and yelp as if terrified by an invisible force. And then there are the dogs who have the opposite reaction, those who wag their tails uncontrollably and jump around with delight. It seems some canines are happy to meet the friendly little ghost dog and just want to play.

Bobby's ghost means no harm. He is not evil or demonic. He's just the spirit of a beloved pet, a loyal friend and companion. Edinburgh honors the memory of Bobby each 14th of January with the official Greyfriars Bobby Day. Whether you believe in ghosts or not, Bobby has managed to live on in the hearts of the Scottish people and dog lovers all over the world. Greyfriars Bobby, the remarkable little dog with a heart of gold, just longs to be reunited with his master. May they remain together in peace and continue the bond of love formed so many years ago.

An interesting side note: Greyfriars Cemetery has earned the reputation as one of the most haunted places in the world! Famous for not only for the ghost of sweet Bobby, but for a more terrifying entity known as the MacKenzie Poltergeist. This violent and vengeful spirit attacks unsuspecting visitors near the famous "black mausoleum" and in an area called the Covenanters Prison. In 1672, George MacKenzie, a cruel man by all accounts, rounded up 1200 poor and religious nonconformists, known as Covenanters, and placed them in a makeshift prison in a section of Greyfriars. Their only crime was not swearing allegiance to King Charles II. George "Bloody" MacKenzie made their lives a living hell. Conditions for these unfortunate souls were unbearable. Many died of exposure, hunger, or dysentery. Others were executed. It was a horrific place of unimaginable suffering. Ironically, after his death, MacKenzie himself was buried nearby.

Today, people report violent attacks, fainting spells, sickness, and other unnatural occurrences near and around the black mausoleum. A very dark paranormal force surrounds the area with a thick blanket of oppression. Apparitions, shadow figures, and a vengeful poltergeist lurk in a dark recess of MacKenzie's tomb. The death of more than one person, including an exorcist, has been attributed to the evil entity that haunts Greyfriars Kirkyard! But those are stories for another day...

Dogs of War

The brave men and women who serve on the front lines and battlefields often leave behind a worried family. They pray fervently for the safe return of their loved one. Unfortunately, sometimes their prayers go unanswered.

The picture of the fallen soldier elicits an all too familiar image. A flag- draped coffin escorted off a plane while a grieving widow comforts bewildered children. A spouse understands the possible consequences when their partner goes to war. A child can be helped through the grieving process. But what of our beloved canine companions? A pet may suffer the same feeling of loss. How are they able to understand this very human emotion? We've all heard the stories. A loyal dog refuses to leave his master's side, even after death. Is it an anomaly? A rare occurrence? Actually, it happens more often than you think...

Hawkeye

It had always been Jon Tumilson's dream to be a Navy Seal. He accepted the potential dangers of the job willingly. He left his family, including his dog, to fight for freedom in a foreign land thousands of miles from his home in Rockford, Iowa. In August of 2011, Tumilson, known as "J.T.," was tragically killed while on assignment in Afghanistan. J.T. was one of many soldiers aboard a Chinook helicopter when it was shot down by a rocket-powered grenade. His death was that of a hero and he was given the funeral befitting a fallen soldier.

Over 1500 mourners gathered at the funeral to pay their respects to the brave Navy Seal. Leading the mourners into the church was Hawkeye, Tumilson's Chocolate Labrador Retriever. Tumilson's loved ones were overwhelmed with grief, as would be expected at such a sad event. The most emotionally distraught member of the family was the dog, Hawkeye, who refused to leave his master's side.

Hawkeye laid despondently at the foot of the casket during the entire service. No one dared move him from his chosen spot. The dog's emotional pain was evident. His sorrowful moans could be heard between prayers, resonating throughout the church. Hawkeye somehow understood what was happening at the service. He was saying goodbye to the most important person in his life: his master, his friend. Hawkeye was as loyal to Tumilson as Tumilson was to his country.

The video of Tumilson's funeral became a viral internet sensation. Besides touching the hearts of patriots and dog lovers, it inspired the producers of the popular television program "NCIS." The CBS show, which centers on the work of the Naval Criminal Investigative Services, aired a special episode about a bomb-sniffing dog whose master was killed by a sniper in Afghanistan. The military funeral scene was said to be inspired from the actual footage of Hawkeye at Tumilson's service. The episode was dedicated to "military working dogs and their brave handlers everywhere."

Theo

Thousands of men and women are called to serve in the armed forces. Occasionally, our four-legged friends are also called into duty. Dogs are employed in many capacities in war zones and on battlefields. These dogs are not pets, but true soldiers who put their lives on the line for the greater good. One such animal was a Springer Spaniel mix named Theo.

Theo was trained to find explosives, a common threat to both soldier and civilian in war-torn countries. Theo's handler was Lance Cpl. Liam Tasker, a British soldier in the Royal Army Veterinary Corps. The pair were inseparable during their tour of duty. Together they had successfully uncovered dozens of deadly bombs, saving countless lives in the process.

In March of 2011, Tasker and Theo came under fire while searching for explosives in Hemland Province in Afghanistan. Tasker was fatally wounded during the battle. Theo, always at his master's side, watched in horror as his partner was brutally gunned down. When the fighting subsided, Theo was found alive but upset, guarding Tasker's lifeless body. The dog died a few hours later after being taken back to the British army base.

Theo was not shot or injured during the firefight. He had no visible wounds. The veterinary staff was at a loss. They could find no obvious cause of death. Military officials said the dog must have suffered a fatal seizure triggered by stress. The chaos of the firefight and death of his partner were too much for the loyal canine.

Those who knew Tasker and Theo believe it was heartbreak that took the dog's life. Although their physical connection was severed, their emotional bond could not be broken. Tasker's family didn't believe a seizure killed the dog. They knew that Theo died of a broken heart and simply refused to go on without his partner. The remains of both were returned to their home in Kirkcaldy, Scotland.

Spectral Cats

Cats, more than any other animal, seem to have perceptive abilities beyond what humans have. They can see in almost complete darkness, have an extraordinary sense of smell, and even know when the weather is about to turn. Call it a sixth sense, a supernatural superpower.

But can they see ghosts? There are hundreds of stories that back up this theory. There's nothing creepier than kitty growling and hissing at something unseen. What is it that makes these creatures act in such a defensive and frightened manner? Can a cat "imagine" a ghost? Can they hallucinate? Or is there something there, just beyond our human perception, that sends these animals into such a state of aggravation. To many, cats are like a paranormal alarm system, warning us of unseen dangers.

On the other side of the coin are the reports of cats that are ghosts. Ghost cats are the most commonly reported form of paranormal animal. It seems they refuse to leave their home even after death. Pet owners claim these phantom felines are more comforting than creepy.

Sentinel, the Lighthouse Cat

A very well-known cat haunts a lighthouse in Fairport Harbor, Ohio. This ghost kitty is so famous it has appeared on national television! Sentinel is the feline phantom that saved a museum.

Captain Joseph Babcock was hired as the head lighthouse keeper in 1871. Captain Babcock, his wife, and two sons lived on the second floor of the keeper's house. The Babcock family experienced tragic times when their young son, Robby, abruptly passed away from an unexpected illness. Mrs. Babcock was never the same. She became bedridden while suffering a deep depression.

Animals have always proven to be of comfort to humans. Captain Babcock showed his concern for his grief-stricken wife by making sure she had plenty of company - in the form of cats.

He knew she had always found solace in her feline companions, and hoped the kitties would alleviate the pain of such a great loss. The small creatures seemed to help Mrs. Babcock cope with her lonely life at the lighthouse.

Sadly, Mrs. Babcock eventually passed away. Many claimed it was a broken heart that took her life. Most of the cats wandered away after their mistress was gone. The Captain took no notice after the devastating death of his wife. But one particular gray cat did linger and was seen on the property for quite some time. With a mournful cry, it went from room to room aimlessly searching for the missing Mrs. Babcock.

Years passed and the Fairport lighthouse eventually became a museum. A full-time curator was hired. She took residence in the Babcock's former living quarters. Soon after moving in, she noticed a small furry gray creature running about in her home. The strange apparition would appear suddenly and disappear just as quickly. It was so upsetting that she brought her concerns before the museum trustees to see if they could help. They could find no rationale for the phenomena and chalked it up to an overactive imagination.

But these frightening sightings continued. One night the curator was startled as she felt something unseen jump onto her bed. She swore it was a cat. Museum visitors began reporting strange happenings as well. Many claimed they had seen small gray wisps of "smoke" while checking out the displays.

In 2001, the museum trustees voted to install a new

heating and cooling unit. A man working on installing new AC vents ran into a slight problem. In order to complete the job, he needed to squeeze into a tight space under the steps of the keeper's house. As he wiggled his way into the dark void, he realized his body was in contact with something that felt quite odd. He grabbed his flashlight to get a look and was horrified to discover the body of a mummified cat!

This preserved gray kitty is considered to be the source of the paranormal activity at the Fairport Harbor lighthouse. The remains of the mummy cat, aptly named Sentinel the ghost cat, can be seen on display at the museum today. The reports of feline hauntings still continue.

Seti Saint John

Cats are mystical creatures. In ancient Egypt, when the family cat passed on, the whole clan went into mourning. Domestic cats were considered deities, and killing a cat was punishable by death. Egyptians believed that animals were crucial to one's spiritual survival. This was based upon how well one treated the animal during their life on earth. Beloved pets were often mummified in order to keep their deceased master company in the afterlife. Goddess cats from Egyptian lore include Baset and Sekhmet.

Friends of ours have always had Sphynx cats as pets. This slender, hairless cat was named the Sphynx because of its resemblance to the cats commonly depicted on ancient hieroglyphics and statuary. This breed of kitty is extraordinarily outgoing and prone to mischief. It seems their special personality continues even in death.

In 2011, Seti the Sphynx cat was rescued by Robert and Barbe Saint John. At the time he was a scared, sick kitty who wouldn't even eat. However, with their constant love and affection, Seti began to thrive. He was a regal and handsome Sphynx, and a constant source of pride for Robert and Barbe. He had many outfits to keep his hairless body warm, fitting for almost any special occasion. At times, Seti's playful ways were exasperating. He would constantly knock things off of tables and chew holes in favorite sweaters. His favorite place to rest was always across Barbe's workstation.

In February of 2017, something went horribly wrong. Seti was sick. It was discovered he had a heart defect that was never correctly identified. The Saint Johns rushed Seti to the vet where the doctors dolefully announced there was nothing to be done. In complete shock, Barbe and Robert watched helplessly as Seti crossed the Rainbow Bridge that day. The grief they suffered in the days and weeks to follow was palpable.

But the spirit of Seti is a strong one. The kitty continues to visit and amuse the Saint John household. Barbe recently posted this encounter on social media: "Seti Saint John finally came to visit me last night. I had a full twenty minutes of hugs and kisses before he vanished. He's too busy exploring his new surroundings to stick around me when he is making sure I'm fine and that's okay. That's how he was here, always looking for something to get into."

A Haunted Horse

A sad tale of love and a ghost begins with a horse. But this isn't a living, breathing horse - this is a beautiful and stately carousel horse, known as Muller's Military Horse. In 1917, Daniel C. Muller, a master carver, was commissioned to create this magnificent wooden carousel stallion. He had a keen eye for detail and the animals he created were said to have perfect proportions.

Muller had always been fascinated with Civil War Cavalry mounts. He wanted to showcase the Military Horse in his design. The horse carved by Muller in his project was nothing short of a masterpiece. It was admired by many, but none more so than his own wife. After glimpsing her husband's amazing creation, Mrs. Muller is said to have fallen deeply in love with the steed. Her jealousy was quite evident and she proclaimed she could not imagine anyone riding the Military Horse, except for herself.

After completion, the carousel and its horses were installed at Cedar Point Amusement Park in Sandusky, Ohio. After her passing, Mrs. Muller's ghost was said to haunt this location. The spectral figure of a woman appeared, descending out of the darkness. It was also reported that the carousel would start up on its own. The park's maintenance crew investigated the mechanics of the carousel, but could never find an apparent reason for it to spontaneously start.

On many nights, long after the park closed, the stately figure of a phantom woman was seen riding the Military Horse. The story holds that this particular horse cannot be properly photographed. Perhaps the spirit of Mrs. Muller prevents anyone from capturing the image of her beloved haunted steed. Sadly, this carousel is no longer on display in the park. The ghostly tale of a phantom horse and its lovestruck rider now belong to the legends of Cedar Point.

FURTHER READING

"American Experience: Murder of the Century." PBS, October 16, 1995 Baker, Jon. "19th Century Love Story Has Happy Ending." *Murderpedia*, November 18, 2002. http://murderpedia.org/male.C/c/carr-thomas.htm

Banim, Julia. "Loyal Dog Dies After Sleeping At Owner's Grave Every Night For 11 Years." *UNILAD,* 22 Feb. 2018, www.unilad.co.uk/animals/loyal-dog-dies-after-sleeping-at-owners-grave- every-night-for-11-years/.

Blanco, Juan Ignacio. "Thomas D.Carr." *Murderpedia*, http://murderpedia.org/male.C/c/carr-thomas.htm

Belanger, Jeff. Conversations and written notes, May 2, 2017

Brandon, Craig. *Grace Brown's Love Letters; and her 1902 diary*. Keene, NH: Surry Cottage Books, 2006

Carr, Thomas D. *Life and Confession of Thomas D. Carr.* St. Clairesville, OH: J.W. Heaton & Co., 1870

"Chester Gillette Hears His Death Sentence With A Smile." *The Post-Standard, Syracuse, NY, December 11, 1906.*

Denny Schultz, Gladys; Gordon Low, Daisy. *Lady From Savannah: The Life of Juliette Low*. Savannah, GA: Girl Scouts of the United States of America; 2nd edition, 1988.

D'Imperio, Chuck. "Murder of Grace Brown: Relive infamous crime at Big Moose Lake in Adirondacks." *New York Upstate*, April 15, 2016. http://www.newyorkupstate.com/ adirondacks/2016/04/grace_brown murder_big_moose_inn_adirondacks_ny_chester_gillette.html

Drazen, Patrick. *A Gathering of Spirits: Japan's Ghost Story Tradition*. iUniverse, 2011

Dutcher, Denise M. *Dead Reckoning; A Great Lakes Love Story.* Author published, 2014.

Edwards, Jeff. "When His Handler Was Killed, This Heroic War Dog Died of a Broken Heart the Same Day." *WAR HISTORY ONLINE*, 21 Jan. 2018, www.warhistoryonline.com/history/handler-killed-war-dog-died- broken-heart.html.

Find A Grave, database and images (http://www.findagrave.com: accessed 29 November 2017), memorial page for Louiza Catharine Fox (8 Feb 1855-21 Jan 1869), Find A Grave Memorial no. 11500870, citing Salem Cemetery, Hendrysburg, Belmont County, Ohio, USA; Maintained by venusblue (contributor 46541949).

Find A Grave, database and images (http://www.findagrave.com: accessed 29 November 2017), memorial page for Mary Jane "Minnie" Quay (May 1861-27 Apr 1876), Find A Grave Memorial no. 13580810, citing Forester Township Cemetery, Carsonville, Sanilac County, Michigan, USA; Maintained by Find A Grave (contributor 8).

Find A Grave, Database and images (http://www.findagrave.com: accessed 29 November 2017), memorial page for Zona "Greenbriar Ghost" Heaster Shue (1876-23 Jan 1897), Find A Grave Memorial no. 5015852, citing Soule Chapel Methodist Cemetery, Meadow Bluff, Greenbrier County, West Virginia, USA; Maintained by Find A Grave.

Hammond, Ambrose "The Ghost and Legend of Minnie Quay." *Michigan's Otherside*, http://michigansotherside.com/the-ghost-and-legend-of- minnie-quay

Harris, Michael; Sickler, Linda. *Historic Haunts of Savannah*.

Charleston, SC: Haunted America, A Division of The History Press, 2014.

Harrison, Ben. *Undying Love.* Marathon, Florida: The Ketch & Yawl Press, 2009.

Henderson, Jan-Andrew, *The Ghost That Haunted Itself.* Mainstream Publishing. July, 2001.

Johnson, Ben. "The Story of Greyfriars Bobby." *Historic UK*, http://www.historic-uk.com/HistoryUK/HistoryofScotland/Greyfriars- Bobby/

Johnston, Laura. "The Ghost Cat of the Fairport Harbor Lighthouse: An Eerie Erie Story." *Rock The Lake,* 3 Nov. 2017, www.rockthelake.com/buzz/2017/10/ghost-cat-fairport-harbor-lighthouse- eerie-erie-story/.

Lessard, Suzannah. *The Architect of Desire: Beauty and Danger in the Stanford White Family.* Delta, 1997.

Lewis, Fairweather. "Willie and Nellie." *Fairweather Lewis* (website), February 12, 2012. https://fairweatherlewis.wordpress.com/2012/02/12/willie-and- nellie/

Longfellow, Henry Wadsworth. *"Tales of a Wayside Inn (Prelude),"* 1863 Longfellow's Wayside Inn, http://www.wayside.org/history

"Malabar Farm." *Forgotten OH*, http://www.forgeottenoh.com/ Counties/Richland/malabar.html

Markel, Dr. Howard. "Doctors Still Argue about This Prince's Early Death." *PBS, Public Broadcasting Service*, 15 Dec. 2017, www.pbs.org/newshour/health/156-years-after-prince-alberts-death-we-still-dont-know-exactly-why-he-died.

McKay, Gretchen. Cambria County mansion rumored to be haunted by ghost of legendary "Gibson Girl,'" Pittsburgh Post-Gazette, October 27, 2001. http://old.post-gazette.com/homes/20011027hauntedhome8p8.asp

"Murder in 1896." *The Lima News*, October 22, 2013. http://www.limaohio.com/archive/28888/news-news_lifestyles-442320-murder-in-1896

Rule, Leslie. *Ghosts among Us: True Stories of Spirit Encounters.* Andrew McMeel Pub., 2004.

Saint John, Barbe. Conversations and notes. August, 2017.

Spencer, Mark. *A Haunted Love Story: The Ghosts of the Allen House*.

Woodbury, Minnesota: Llewellyn Publications, 2012.

Stiles, Kristina. *The History of Grace Brown.* 1996.

Sykes, Tom. "How John Brown Was Queen Victoria's Channel to Albert's Ghost." *The Daily Beast,* The Daily Beast Company, 13 June 2013, www.thedailybeast.com/how-john-brown-was-queen-victorias-channel-to- alberts-ghost.

Quackenbush, Jannette Rae. "Belmont County Ohio Ghosts and Hauntings - Louisa Fox Murder Site." *Ohio Ghost Hunter Guide,* http://hauntedhocking.com/Haunted_Ohio_Belmont_County_Louisa_Fox_Murder_Site.htm

Rodgers, Garry. "How A Ghost's Evidence Convicted A Murderer." *DyingWords.ne*t, February 13, 2016. http://dyingwords.net/how-a-ghosts- evidence-convicted-a-murderer/

Roper, Matt. "Loyal Dog Ran Away from Home to Find His Dead Master's Grave - and Has Stayed by Its Side for Six Years." *Daily Mail Online, Associated Newspapers,* 13 Sept. 2012, www.dailymail.co.uk/news/article- 2202509/Loyal-dog-ran-away-home-dead-masters-grave--stayed-years.html.

Rush, Chris. "Haunted Ross Castle And The Black Baron." *Spooky Isles*, http://spookyisles.com/2017/04/haunted-ross-castle/

Santore, Beth. "Malabar Farm, Lucas, Ohio." *Grave*

Addiction, http://www.graveaddiction.com/malabar.html

Tabler, Dave. "The Greenbrier Ghost." *Appalachian History*, January 29, 2015. http://www.appalachianhistory.net/2015/01/greenbrier-ghost.html

The Legend of Minnie Quay." *Travel Channel, Dead Files, Season 2, Episode 11*, 2012. http://www.travelchannel.com/videos/legend-of-minnie-quay-0192370

"The Tragic Story of Celia "Ceely" Rose." *News Journal*, Mansfield, OH, October 9, 2003.

Trueman, C N. "Henry VIII and Ireland." *The History Learning Site*, March 17, 2015. http://www.historylearningsite.co.uk/tudor-england/henry-viii-and-ireland/

Uruburu, Paula. *American Eve: Evelyn Nesbit, Stanford White, the Birth of the "It" Girl, and the Crime of the Century*. Riverhead Books, 2008.

Venning, Annabel. "Did Queen Victoria Talk to the Ghost of Her Darling Albert? A New Book Says the Grieving Queen Held Bizarre Seances - with Her 'Lover' John Brown Channelling the Dead Prince's Spirit." *Daily Mail Online*, Associated Newspapers, 26 Dec. 2013, http://www.dailymail.co.uk/news/article-2529294/Did-Queen-Victoria-talk- ghost-darling-Albert-A-new-book-says-grieving-Queen-held-bizarre-seances-lover-John-Brown-channelling-dead-Princes-spirit.html.

Wells, Charlie. "Argentinian Dog Stays by His Master's Grave for Six Years - NY Daily News." Nydailynews.com, *New York Daily News*, 13 Sept. 2012, www.nydailynews.com/news/world/argentinian-dog-stays-master- grave-years-article-1.1159250.

West Virginia Division of Culture and History. "The Greenbrier Ghost." http://www.wvculture.org/history/

notewv/ghost.html
Willis, James. *The Big Book of Ohio Ghost Stories.*
Mechanicsburg, PA: Stackpole Books, 2013.

ABOUT THE AUTHORS

Theresa Argie and **Cathi Weber**, aka The Haunted Housewives, have traveled the world in search of ghosts, urban legends, and mysteries of the unknown. They view the paranormal from the historic perspective. Their adage is, "A bad day of ghost-hunting can still be a good day of history!" Theresa is an award-winning author and speaker who has been pursuing the paranormal for decades. Cathi, owner of the renowned Willoughby Ghost Walk, is an accomplished author and historian with a knack for clever storytelling. The Haunted Housewives are more than just ghost hunters, they are champions of the past. They strive to preserve the memories of those who came before, tell their stories, and give a voice to the dead.

Made in the USA
Columbia, SC
04 September 2018